LOVE
Relationships

A Moving Sea

LOVE
Relationships

A Moving Sea

Charles Thomas Cayce
&
Leslie Goodman Cayce

ARE
PRESS

**ASSOCIATION FOR
RESEARCH AND
ENLIGHTENMENT**

A.R.E. Press • Virginia Beach • Virginia

A.R.E. Press
Sixty-Eighth & Atlantic Avenue
P.O. Box 656
Virginia Beach, VA 23451-0656

Library of Congress Cataloging-in-Publication Data
Cayce, Charles Thomas, 1942-
    Love relationships : a moving sea / by Charles Thomas
Cayce and Leslie Goodman Cayce.
        p.   cm.
    Includes bibliographical references.
    ISBN 0-87604-347-3
    1. Love. 2. Man-woman relationships. 3. Interpersonal
relations. 4. Cayce, Edgar, 1877-1945. Edgar Cayce readings.
I. Cayce, Leslie Goodman, 1953- . II. Title.
BF1045.L7C38   1995
158'.2—dc20   95-30994

Biblical quotes are from the Revised Standard Version.

Cover design by Richard Boyle

*We dedicate this endeavor to
Sally and Hugh Lynn, Bob and Eleanor*

. . . you shall be together even in the silent
memory of God.
But let there be spaces in your togetherness,
And let the winds of the heavens dance between
you.

Love one another, but make not a bond of love:
Let it rather be a moving sea between the shores
of your souls.
Fill each other's cup but drink not from one cup.
Give one another of your bread but eat not of the
same loaf.
Sing and dance together and be joyous, but let
each one of you be alone,
Even as the strings of a lute are alone though they
quiver with the same music.

Give your hearts, but not into each other's keep-
ing.
For only the hand of Life can contain your hearts.
And stand together yet not too near together:
For the pillars of the temple stand apart,
And the oak tree and the cypress grow not in each
other's shadow.

The Prophet, Kahlil Gibran

Contents

Foreword

*T*his book, *Love Relationships,* draws upon the advice Edgar Cayce gave to many people who sought his advice about their marriages, their families, their friendships. In addition to focusing on the concepts from the Cayce readings that pertain to committed relationships, we have described how my wife, Leslie, and I have tried to apply these concepts in our own marriage and in relationships with our two children, our parents, and other loved ones.

Leslie is a medical social worker and my field was psychology before I assumed administrative duties at the A.R.E.

We lecture on committed relationships and have conducted workshops for couples.

We hope our book will offer you some helpful new insights toward making your own love relationships more personally gratifying and soul satisfying.

Charles Thomas Cayce, Ph.D.
President
Association for Research and Enlightenment, Inc.

Introduction

The Pearls from the Oyster

*H*ow many married couples do you personally know who are truly happy and loving in their relationship? Scores? A dozen or so? Or can you count them on the fingers of one hand? To live lovingly with another person or a family is not easy. Most of us, thank goodness, are persistent optimists and continue to believe that *this* person and *this* relationship or *that* circumstance will not only be different, but also better than others we may have come in contact with. In this flush of new hope, marriages and children are born.

All of the world's major religions suggest at their root that our purpose in life is to come to love God with all our heart, mind, and soul and to love our neighbor as ourselves. In fact, the Cayce readings suggest that our love for God is demonstrated daily by the love we express in our human relationships. Simply stated, if we do not love one another, we do not love God.

Even in a relationship, each of us seems to be encased in an individual oyster shell of circumstance, capability, and personality. Yet our daily struggle with the nitty-gritty sand of events and interactions affords us the unique potential to create within ourselves the priceless gem of unsurpassed beauty. Our pearl of love is shaped and polished by our encounters with opportunities for intimacy, communicating, serving one another, and sharing.

To make the struggle even more interesting, the issue of relationships is charged with paradox: Becoming as one in love and spirit, yet remaining as two in identity and individuality; and the need to know oneself before truly knowing another. Also paradoxically, although a relationship takes on a kind of life of its own and may seem to create its own shared and shining jewel, the pearls are formed independently within the separate shells of each individual. Not all oysters produce pearls; not all relationships sustain love.

Just as the pearl may be created by the oyster's response to the irritating friction from grating particles, love in each of the persons in a relationship deepens and gains strength according to how each deals with the friction that is an inevitable byproduct of the intimacy of a relationship. Friction alone is obviously not love-producing. How each person responds to it and works with it determines the quality of the love within the relationship, as well as within each individual.

The unattractive, misshapen shell of the oyster deserves a special tribute in our metaphor. Its rough surface, its irregular shape, and its plain colors remind us of our own qualities that may not all be admirable, especially as displayed in a relationship. Rough edges, surface bumpiness, and even the occasional appearance of dullness are unavoidable in any close relationship simply because of the intimate involvement of two imperfect individuals. In this book, we have chosen not to minimize these oyster-shell qualities. We chose to respect them, neither dwelling on them nor ignoring them.

When we look at some of our model love relationships of the past—perhaps those of our parents or grandparents—we have to wonder: Has it become more difficult in recent years to live lovingly in a relationship?

The psychic readings of Charles Thomas's grandfather, Edgar Cayce, refer to the years between 1958 and 1998 as a period of accelerating world changes. As this is being written, we take note of obvious changes in national political systems, the planetary environment, and medical technology, for example. Many transformations during this period are cultural rather than physical, but they have no less an impact on how we live today. Two such trends—changing attitudes about sexual practices and changing views of the roles of women in our society—have a direct impact on the nature and nurture of our relationships.

Sexual attitudes moved from the conservative values of the 1950s to the extreme permissiveness of the 1960s; after a period of reassessment, the 1980s and early 1990s represented a somewhat less liberal position regarding sexual activity, partly as a reaction to the incidence of AIDS. This modest retreat has been accompanied, however, by greater exposure to information on such previously taboo topics as sexual abuse, homosexuality, and sexual addiction. The fact that sex is openly discussed and frequently alluded to or portrayed in print, recordings, radio, television, and the movies means that attitudes and understandings about sex—and love relationships—are being continually assailed.

During the same period, the perceived and accepted roles of women have evolved in the beneficial direction of greater independence, with greater opportunity lagging slightly behind. Women now play a much more significant role in the work force, which in turn modifies their role in the structure of the traditional home. That same independence, combined with the trends on sexual information, has also contributed to an increase in the number of divorces and a decrease in the acceptance of the traditional values of making or keeping a commitment in a love relationship.

As an outgrowth of such social and individual changes, we believe it has become even more difficult, more complicated than ever, to establish and maintain a healthy love relationship. The need for constructive guidance on relationships seems greater than ever before. This book attempts to help meet this need by presenting ideas from the Cayce readings on building healthy relationships and healing difficult ones.

Edgar Cayce gave readings for approximately 6,000 people, many of whom asked about relationships. Perhaps 3,000 of the over 14,000 readings contain advice on this critical aspect of our lives. We—Leslie and Charles Thomas— have applied many of these concepts in our own lives and in our professional work with individuals, couples, and groups in counseling, lectures, and workshops. This book is both a review of the Edgar Cayce information on relationships and a report of our experiences in applying that information in our love relationship.

We allowed ourselves to approach the writing of this book individually, according to our personalities, perspectives, and writing styles. Leslie's contributions (Parts II and III) are portrayals of our attempts to implement specific ideas from the readings in our marriage; Charles Thomas presents a philosophical context for considering relationships (Part I), deals with three especially sensitive issues in love relationships (Part III), and presents suggestions for a series of activities ("projects") designed to strengthen relationships. Although the focus of these projects is on marriage relationships and other one-to-one love relationships between two adults, many of the ideas are applicable to relationships with our children, our parents, our siblings, our friends, and our co-workers—in other words, to all the relationships in our lives.

Writing about our relationship—like the relationship itself—has not been easy, smooth, or ever harmonious. The book represents where we are now—very much in process, in the midst of grappling with our opportunities and striving to implement the tools we have found. Therefore, this is not a comprehensive manual on marriage or love relationships; we do not have all the answers. Rather, the ideas continue to challenge and awaken us to deeper potentials for giving to the relationship. If we have effectively translated any of that experience and awareness to the printed page, the book's purpose will have been met.

Charles Thomas Cayce
Leslie Goodman Cayce

Part I

A Philosophy
of Relationships

— Charles Thomas Cayce —

1

⚜️

Relationships as
the Homeward Path

Consider for a moment how much of your life involves your relationships with other people: living with them, working with them, giving service to them, getting service from them, communicating with them, having fun with them, worrying about them. Think about a recent "typical" day and estimate what percentage of your waking hours you were directly interacting with another person or people. Add to that the amount of time you spent alone, but in activities necessitated by your relationships with others. What's the total? Fifty percent? Seventy? Ninety? Unless you live a very solitary existence, relationship activity probably consumes a significant majority of your time.

Some people live for relationship activity. They consider themselves "people people" and relish the daily encounters with other human beings, applying the full range of their skills and abilities to be successful in their relationships. Such people are often attracted to careers such as sales, teaching, nursing, supervising, and counseling. Less frequently recognized are the needs for effective relationship skills in parenting and in being a partner in a marriage or other love relationship.

Individuals who are not quite so people oriented—and even "people people" now and then—relish the time when they do not have to relate to others. In fact, just as we need a balance among other aspects of our lives, a balance between relationships activity and private time is essential to our overall state of well-being.

Furthermore, as individuals become more aware of their spiritual nature and undertake serious study of spiritual philosophy—such as that represented by the Edgar Cayce readings—they often find themselves frustrated by the limited amount of time they have for such study. It is not unusual for such a new seeker to push aside as many responsibilities for relationship activity as possible—especially those around the home. In frustration, such an eager person might say, "If I could only forget about all these time-consuming relationships, I'd have more time to spend on my spiritual enlightenment and development." It is not unusual for even experienced seekers of spiritual truths to want time off from dealing with some relationships in their lives.

The paradox is that our relationships are probably the most important means we each have for exploring and developing our spirituality.

Relationships: School for Spiritual Lessons

As part of the Pharisees' challenge to His ministry, Jesus was asked, " . . . which is the great commandment in the law?" Jesus answered, "You shall love the Lord your God with all your heart, and with all your soul, and with all your mind. This is the great and first commandment. And a second is like it, You shall love your neighbor as yourself. On these two commandments depend all the law and the prophets." (Matthew 22:36-40)

The Cayce readings frequently remind us of this teaching and its implication: We have no greater responsibility than to *love*—first to love God and then to love one another as ourself. This puts the highest possible priority on our relationships. In fact, the readings go further by telling us that the quality of our relationships with others represents the quality of our relationship with God. In other words, if I want to know how I stand with God, I can look at my relationships with others. If I am experiencing difficulties in my personal relationships, then I am experiencing difficulties in my relationship with God. If we need more practice and testing of our ability to love—fully and unconditionally, for example—our relationships within the family provide plenty of opportunities.

The teachings of Jesus encourage us to stretch ourselves when they say that we must love our enemies. The Cayce readings elaborate on this idea by stating our ability to love one another is not really proven on those who also love us; the test is with those who appear to dislike us or who are stumbling blocks in our lives. The readings go even further to say that we have an ongoing responsibility toward the spiritual progress of others, particularly by setting an example in our own lives. One way that is to be carried out is represented by the often cited, often-neglected Golden Rule: "As ye would that [others] should do to you, do ye even so to them." (Edgar Cayce reading 5347-2)[1]

So can we set aside our relationships for a time and concentrate instead on our spiritual development? Literally, not on your life! In today's parlance, relationships "is where it's at."

If we choose to ignore these injunctions about relationships or even about spiritual development, what difference does it really make? To answer that requires an expanded view of our relationships to the universe and to God.

A Cosmic View of Relationships

The view presented here emerges from the Edgar Cayce readings, establishing the concept that we are children of God on a path toward ultimate oneness with God. The view provides a useful theoretical framework for considering some of the dynamics of relationships in subsequent discussions.

The Creation of Souls, the Christ Pattern, and Christ Consciousness. Everything that exists originated in God, who is often referred to in the readings as the Creative Force or the Universal Source. Out of a desire for companionship and expression, God created *souls* much like Himself ("in His own image"), intending for the souls to be co-creators with Him. Every soul embraced God's indelible imprint in the form of the *Christ pattern.* That pattern signifies the soul's oneness with the Creator.

At creation, every soul had full awareness of its union with God and its existence as one of His children. This

---

[1]The more than 14,000 readings given by Edgar Cayce are numbered to facilitate reference and research. The number before the hyphen represents the individual for whom the reading was given; the identity of individuals is thus protected. The number behind the hyphen represents which reading was given for the individual. Reading 5347-2, then, is the second reading that was given for the individual who was assigned number 5347. All further references to the readings in this volume will be followed by such a reading number.

awareness of oneness with the Father is referred to in the readings as *the universal Christ Consciousness.* Through it, each soul had complete, direct experience of divine love both for itself and toward other souls.

Each soul was also given the quality of *free will,* allowing the soul to choose whether to act in harmony with the love and the will of God or to act according to other soul-created motives. When a soul acted in ways contrary to God's imprint (the Christ pattern), the soul's awareness of its oneness with God (its Christ Consciousness) became dimmed. Repeated rebellion against God's will caused the Christ Consciousness to become dormant.

Some souls did choose not to follow God's will. A number of these were attracted to the earth, which had been evolving as a three-dimensional manifestation of God's creative spirit. They involved themselves in physical aspects of the earth that were incompatible with divine love. Those souls began to take on physical forms, losing sight of their spiritual nature and their intended relationship to God. Eventually, the souls that associated themselves with a physical form could no longer voluntarily withdraw from the earth. (This transformation from purely spiritual form to physical form is referred to in some theories as "The Fall.")

God's imprint of the Christ pattern in the souls was never lost, although the Christ Consciousness was dimmed or temporarily extinguished in the earthbound beings. Each of the earth beings, which have evolved into humans over the eons of earth's history, has one of the rebel souls. Since God is love and is loving of all souls, regardless of their misuse of free will, He provides a way for the souls to return to God as co-creators. Human beings can always begin acting in ways that reawaken them to full participation in divine love. The earth provides the opportunities to learn and practice those ways.

Reincarnation. If we had only a single lifetime on earth

in which to perfect this process of spiritual development and return to the Father, probably none of us would make it. But God in His infinite wisdom and understanding has not placed any limit on our earthly experiences. Through reincarnation, we are given as many chances as we need to learn the Christ pattern and to express it in our earthly lives. To help us, God has sent to earth from time to time an individual to teach and to demonstrate the pattern as it applies to humanity. The soul-messenger from God has appeared in several incarnations, including Adam, Jacob's son Joseph, Joshua, and Jesus.

At each physical death, the soul survives. It may then spend time in nonphysical realms of experience for other learning, and it may return for another experience as a human being. Everything that happens to us in each life is recorded within the soul, usually out of reach of the conscious mind of the human, who is mainly concerned with the events of the current lifetime. However, each lifetime for a particular soul is influenced by those lives that the soul experienced before it. The influence may be helpful, taking advantage of past learning and spiritual progress, or the influence may be distracting with the potential of being harmful. One mechanism by which these carryovers from one life to another take place is known as *karma*.

Karma and Grace.   From the perspective of the Edgar Cayce readings, karma can be understood most readily as the law of cause and effect in action. Every exercise of the will is a cause, and the action that results is an effect. To some people, karma has a negative connotation, implying a form of divine retribution for misdeeds of a past life. Through the law of karma, however, we experience not only the unpleasant consequences of our selfish, misdirected choices, but also the positive outcomes of our loving choices. The effects may be within the same lifetime, as the cause, or in a later lifetime. Through karma, we learn which types of choices bring us closer to God and which ones increase our sense of separation from Him, sometimes referred to as "sin."

When the effects are carried over into a subsequent lifetime, we may find it difficult to realize how we ourselves have created the circumstances in which we find ourselves. Pleasant or unpleasant as our situation might be, it had its cause in our own past choices and actions.

The law of karma through cause and effect is mitigated by the power of *grace*. Grace begins in God's eternal love for each of us—as souls and as human beings. It is not earned through our actions, but bestowed as an aspect of God's divine forgiveness. Through grace we receive God's direct help in meeting the consequences of our past misuse of free will. Grace helps us overcome the habitual weaknesses we have developed through self-interested actions, and grace can alleviate the karmic results of those actions. It is always available to us if we will but choose to accept it and to live our lives in ways compatible with the Christ pattern.

Karma and grace, then, help us to achieve our purpose for being on the earth—to learn and practice the Christ pattern of love and to make our wills one with the will of God. When these lessons have been learned, it will no longer be necessary for us to return for additional lives.

Past-Life Relationships. Souls often choose to reincarnate in the same pairs, small groups, or even large groups whom they had been a part of during earlier lifetimes. They tend to be attracted to recurrent situations that allow memories from the distant past to be reactivated. We need not meet our karmic memories among the same souls who were present when those memories were formed; however, it seems that we often experience the effects of past choices most efficiently and effectively if the same souls are involved again.

This is part of the explanation of why, according to the

Cayce readings, relationships do not occur by chance. Some of our relationships are renewals of past-life relationships, although the roles may be significantly changed. Our souls are often drawn into potentially helpful relationships. This process is at work when a baby is about to be born into the earth.

Soul's Choice of Circumstances. Many Edgar Cayce readings tell of the prospective parents being a channel for an incoming soul—a soul that has already lived many lifetimes and brings with it certain qualities, patterns, and karma. The readings say that the soul chooses and is "attracted to" the particular circumstances into which it will enter—one that will best suit its individual spiritual development. Thus, the home environment that a couple provides, together with their thoughts, attitudes, and ideals—even prior to conception of a child—have a profound effect on the type of soul likely to be attracted to and choosing the couple.

The idea that there is more than heredity, environment, and chance involved in having children is both exciting and awesome for many prospective parents. They may realize that the setting they create by their actions, thoughts, and attitudes as they prepare to have a child helps determine the soul to be drawn into that family. This underscores the great importance of proper preparation for parenthood, with careful consideration of physical, mental, *and* spiritual matters. The Cayce readings emphasize the crucial role of the parents' spiritual motivation. One couple, who indicated their serious intent to become parents, was told, "This should be that purpose—to each fulfill that purpose the divine influence, God, has for thee." (341-48) In this way, they would make it possible that " . . . the type soul will be given thee that is in keeping with thy abilities to contribute to mankind, to the world, the channel for a soul needed in the present." (341-48)

A vivid description of the whole preparation process is given in the Cayce material on the Essenes, a group of people seeking to provide a suitable environment for the coming of the specific soul that became Jesus. This group exercised great care in guiding the thoughts and actions of the potential parents and of everyone with whom they interacted. Of course, unusual circumstances characterized this event, but the readings clearly imply that most of the same general principles and processes are involved in the reentry of any soul into the earth.

Years ago, I had two experiences involving relationships and the soul's choice of the situation into which it will be born. At the time, I was wrestling with questions about the applicability of reincarnation to everyday life when these two events occurred. Both concerned relationships between young people and their parents.

The first incident occurred when a psychiatrist friend asked me to talk with a teenage girl who had been in a mental hospital for several months, unable or unwilling to communicate with anyone except the psychiatrist. In her conversations with me, the teenager reported overhearing a conversation between her parents that revealed she had been adopted. This news was so painful to her, she said, that she "got out of the real world." It was that experience that prompted her to avoid communicating with others.

She also told of hearing about reincarnation from a volunteer who visited the hospital. The girl became quite interested in the subject and its relevance in her own life. She was impressed by the idea that the soul chooses or is attracted to situations especially suited to its growth at a particular time. It led her to accept the possibility that she—her soul—had chosen the conditions resulting in her adoption and that she was not a helpless victim of circumstances.

After more discussions about this idea and its implications for her, she was released from the hospital. Several months later, I saw this girl, who was then working on a healthy relationship with her family, including the fact that she was adopted. She accepted this painful part of her life when she understood that her soul had been drawn to it for its opportunities for growth.

The second experience involved another teenage girl who stopped at the A.R.E.[2] as she was hitchhiking south from Boston. On my way to noontime staff meditation, I saw her standing in the hallway outside my office, looking at displays on Cayce and the A.R.E. I introduced myself and asked if she would like to go to meditation and then to lunch with several co-workers and me. She agreed. During lunch, the girl talked about how reincarnation might work.

After lunch, she accompanied me on some errands and, in the car, described her recent situation. Living at home in Boston with her parents, she was doing well in high school, but she was using a lot of drugs. When her family tried to stop her drug abuse—her father becoming increasingly angry and violent with her—she moved out, first staying with a friend. When that didn't work out, she dropped out of school and decided to hitchhike around the country.

She stopped at Virginia Beach because she had strong positive memories of living there with her parents when she was very young. In fact, she wanted to find the house in which she had lived, describing a large stucco house with a magnolia tree in the yard. I remembered such a dwelling in the neighborhood where I had delivered papers as a boy. As we drove to look for the house, she asked questions about reincarnation and the idea that the soul chooses situations as special growth opportunities. When we passed the house, she felt she recognized it and cried with happiness at the memories of some of those earlier experiences. As we drove

---

[2]The Association for Research and Enlightenment in Virginia Beach, Virginia, is dedicated to providing those interested with the information in the Edgar Cayce readings through conferences, publications, and other activities.

back to the main street, she continued to cry softly to herself. When we stopped at a traffic light, she suddenly looked up and said she was going home. Before I could respond, she had gotten out of the car, crossed the street, and stuck out her thumb. That was the last I saw of her—heading north.

Several months later, she wrote to say she was at home and back in school; later she again wrote that she had finished high school, and still later that she was in medical school. She said that the possibility that her soul had chosen her particular family and situation in life was real enough to encourage her to take a closer look at her relationships with those around her. She felt that her consideration of reincarnation enabled her to take responsibility for the circumstances of her life, instead of putting the blame somewhere else.

Accepting responsibility for our life situation, including our relationships, is one of the most helpful ways of working with the idea of reincarnation.

Principles of Loving Relationships

Some relationships are brief and distant, as in serving a customer or talking with someone at a party. Others are long-term and close, such as those with spouses and other loved ones. And there's everything in between, such as co-workers, regular clients or customers, neighbors current and from the past, school friends, and whoever the special few may be whom you consider your closest friends. The nature of a relationship, its extent, and its closeness all determine some of the specific skills and actions needed to make the relationship work. Obviously, many thoughts and actions in a relationship are different when the person is a customer or client than when the person is a longtime friend. And each of these relationships require something different from your relationship with your father or mother.

In spite of such differences, however, being successful in any or all of your relationships results from applying a set of common principles and fundamental skills.

The Edgar Cayce readings are a rich source of information and guidance on how to demonstrate the Christ pattern of love in all our relationships. Several of the most significant of these principles and suggestions are presented here.

First Know Self. Because relationships are opportunities to satisfy one's own needs as well as to attend to the needs of others, a fundamental starting point for healthy, loving relationships is knowing oneself. Such knowledge may not come easily, because we all have such effective mechanisms for being selective in our understanding of ourselves and for portraying our qualities in the best possible light. If, for example, I bring to my relationships a strong need for perfection and orderliness, possibly developed and reinforced in past lives as well as in this life, I must recognize how that quality and personal need will affect my relationships. With self-understanding, I may not change my attitudes about perfection for myself, but I may be able to resist expecting perfection from the other parties to my relationships. If I cannot at least do this, I had better limit my relationships to other perfectionists with the same standards I have!

A brief anecdote illustrates this point: A man and a woman were discussing their long-term relationship and its history of disagreements and opportunities:

"Our problem," he said, "starts with the fact that I have very high standards for perfection, and you don't."

"I agree completely," she responded. "That's why you chose me and I chose you."

The process of acquiring self-knowledge is not necessarily one of undergoing psychological or psychiatric counseling, although such services may be helpful. Critical self-observation is a key part of serious spiritual study that includes meditation and prayer and can result in all the self-awareness—and self-change—necessary for being a party to healthy relationships.

The significance of self-knowledge in loving relationships cannot be ignored. Edgar Cayce said that everyone's greatest enemy and worst fault is "self" and that "when self has found self," loving relationships are more likely to be the natural outcome, inspired by a spiritual focus. This leads to the next fundamental concept for relationships—*ideals*.

Ideals. Perhaps the most frequently mentioned idea in the Edgar Cayce readings is the concept of the personal ideal. The ideal represents an individual standard which each person has—knowingly or unknowingly—and by which the person makes choices and evaluates resulting actions and outcomes. The ideal has its foundation at the *spiritual* level with standards such as "peace," "loving service," and "unconditional love." It also has its counterparts at the *mental* level (e.g., desiring to find peaceful solutions to controversy and noticing opportunities for service) and at the *physical* level (e.g., performing acts of service and expressing loving feelings in relationships). As discussed in later chapters, ideals can be established for the relationship itself in addition to the ideals held by each individual.

An understanding of what you hold as your ideal—consciously or unconsciously—directly affects your role and your actions in a relationship. In answer to a question about what the nature of a relationship with a specific person should be, Cayce replied that "This depends upon the ideals and the purposes as may be set for each. They *can* become a helpful influence one to the other, or a great stumbling stone." (2080-1) Another reading states that no one "becomes a part of [your] experience save as an opportunity for the developing of [what you] hold as [your] ideal."

(1581-2) Many other Cayce readings concerning relationships emphasize the importance of having clear ideals established and of making choices of actions and reactions in the relationship in accord with those ideals.

A key concept in the readings related to the ideal is the idea of *purpose*—that each of us has come into this lifetime with a specific spiritual purpose. One of our tasks in spiritual growth is to identify that purpose and then focus our energies toward its fulfillment.

Chance Relationships.   The readings tell us over and over that "Individuals do not meet by chance." (2751-1) All such encounters and relationships are necessary for our development in this life experience, although we may not always use these opportunities in a spiritual manner. One of our responsibilities, Cayce points out, is to use each relationship constructively for spiritual development so that each party is better for having been drawn into the relationship. Acceptance of this concept can have significant impact on the way we act, not only in seemingly casual and accidental relationships, but more important in our long-term relationships with which we may have frequent challenges. Where we do have choices of cultivating friendships and relationships—especially marriage partners—Cayce urges us to search for those who also understand their spiritual purpose, who are trying to apply the Christ pattern in their lives, and who are seeking to reawaken their Christ Consciousness.

Fruits of the Spirit.   This phrase from the apostle Paul's Letter to the Galatians embodies qualities of the Christ pattern such as "love, joy, peace, patience, kindness, goodness, faithfulness, gentleness, self-control . . . " (Galatians 5:22-23) Many of the Cayce readings respond to questions about relationships by suggesting actions based on these loving ideas, "so may one feeding upon the fruits of the spirit come to know that which is love." (272-7) Some of Cayce's most frequent responses, even in situations of apparently bitter conflict, were admonishments to be kind, be gentle, and be patient.

Service to Others. If relationships provide opportune settings for spiritual development, service to others provides an opportune medium for action, both for developing loving qualities such as fruits of the spirit and for applying those qualities in relationships. Cayce's suggestions relative to service range from habitually performing little acts of kindness to shut-ins and the despondent, all the way to helping those who display animosity toward you. You may even have to force yourself to do something you don't like, if it is truly of aid to the other person. Obviously, acts of service—often referred to by Cayce as "being a channel of blessing to others"—should be undertaken for their own sake rather than for anticipated recognition or repayment. Cayce frequently recommends service as the primary means for achieving true happiness in this life.

Attitudes and Emotions. The Cayce readings include a gold mine of insights and suggestions on the frailties of human emotions and the attitudes we carry. I have received letters from thousands of people who have found guidance for their personal difficulties in attitudes and emotions from the Cayce readings. Illustrative of the special insights to be gained from the Cayce material are these:

- What you find as faults in another person are likely to be faults reflected in yourself.
- Poor are those who never show anger; worse are those who cannot control it.
- Forgiveness is only part of a spiritual response to perceived wrongs; the other part of it is forgetting.
- The person who holds resentment owes a lot to the person against whom the resentment is directed.
- In selecting your responses to a disagreement or

conflict, remember you have to live with yourself long
after the other person has left the scene.

- The less one treasures one's own opinions and
listens more to others, the greater the opportunities
for being of help to others.

For more detailed discussion of such provocative ideas,
the reader may find other books published by the A.R.E.
Press to be helpful. Extensive verbatim excerpts from the
Edgar Cayce readings on attitudes and emotions and other
subjects are available in the Library Series.

Against this chapter's background on our full range of relationships, including our relationship to God, we will now
focus in on one specific type of human relationship—the
love relationship.

2

☙

On Marriage

*I*f we are to learn our required spiritual lessons, we will learn that all relationships are loving relationships. One kind of relationship, however, deserves our special attention here—the relationship between husband and wife. While we will discuss and illustrate the love relationship primarily through the experience of marriage, most of the principles apply as well to other committed relationships.

A relationship between a man and a woman can contribute to spiritual growth in a unique way. According to the Edgar Cayce material, sexual energy is an aspect of the universal creative force we call God. This creative power can be used not only in sexual activity, but also in other endeavors. Thus, a love relationship that stimulates the flow of this energy can enhance creativity throughout the lives of the partners to the relationship. Through their relationship, two people have an exceptional opportunity for "expressing the beauty and love of the Creative Forces, or God . . . " (5747-3) These words—part of Edgar Cayce's answer to a question about sexual practices—carry a suggestion both of attunement to our Creator and of love for one another. Together, a man and a woman can progress toward their ultimate purpose in life and reunion with God.

How do we love God in another person? We love the good in that person and build on that good. We love the growth and change in the other person. We love the lawfulness of that growth, and we love God's laws as they manifest in other people. As we pay attention to and magnify the properties of love and of God in the other person, we magnify and build those same properties in ourselves as well.

Love relationships provide an excellent setting in which to learn and apply the fruits of the spirit. They tend to engender in us feelings of kindness and gentleness toward a loved one, and they help us to learn cooperation as we work toward common goals. The experience of living together on a day-to-day basis is also likely, even in the smoothest of relationships, to produce occasions that call for learning and practicing tolerance, patience, and self-control.

The love relationship gives us a paradoxical choice: On the one hand, with a love partner close by, we have *more* opportunities to grow moment by moment and day by day more loving by consciously working at growing more loving to one another. On the other hand, as months and years go by, love partners may begin to take their relationship for granted and put *less* effort into expressing love for each other. Keeping a relationship alive with love requires finding ways to build the lifelong pattern of expressing love between the partners—a worthy reflection of the love of God.

If we follow the Cayce suggestion that we seek partners who are also committed to spiritual growth, the support of that partner can go a long way to help us persevere in overcoming our lacks and building on our best qualities. The joy of sharing our experiences with someone we love can make it easier to become aware of the presence of God and to feel a sincere gratitude for the gift of this life. This in turn can awaken our desire to serve our Creator with our whole being.

"Love" in a Relationship

One of the most familiar portrayals of the qualities of love is found in the apostle Paul's First Letter to the Corinthians:

> Love is patient and kind; love is not jealous or boastful; it is not arrogant or rude. Love does not insist on its own way; it is not irritable or resentful; it does not rejoice at wrong, but rejoices in the right. Love bears all things, believes all things, hopes all things, endures all things. (I Corinthians 13:4-7)

In Erich Fromm's classic work, *The Art of Loving*, the author says that "mature love is union under the condition of preserving one's integrity, one's individuality. It is a state of intensity, awakeness, enhanced vitality which can only be the result of productive and active orientation in many other spheres of life. This allows us to have an 'active concern' for the life and growth of that which we love."

Fromm's idea is that each of us can experience this kind of love only when we have reached the point of feeling whole and secure as a person. Without this sense of wholeness, our balance is disturbed, and we become dependent on others and lose our sense of identity. We often react to these feelings of imbalance and dependency with an energy and intensity that startles or irritates our partner.

In *The Psychology of C. G. Jung,* the author Jakoby says that with the type of wholeness described above there is an "inner freedom which means that a love relation can no longer fetter us; the other sex has lost its magic power over us, for we have come to know its essential traits in the depths of our own psyche. We shall not easily 'fall in love,' for we can no longer lose ourselves to someone else, but we shall be capable of a deeper love, conscious devotion to the other."

Poet Rainer Maria Rilke says this about love: "I hold this to be the highest task of a bond between two people: That each should stand guard over the solitude of the other. For if it lies in the nature of indifference and of the crowd to recognize no solitude, then love and friendship are there for the purpose of continually providing the opportunity for solitude . . .

"[For one human being to love another:] That is perhaps the most difficult of all tasks, the ultimate, the last test in proof, the work for which all other work is but preparation."

Love is one of the principal themes throughout the Edgar Cayce readings. Its centrality to the philosophy of spiritual growth is represented by such statements as, "What is truth? Law! What is Law? Love. What is love? God. What is God? Law and love." (3574-2)

Here are a few of the ideas about love emphasized in the readings:

- "Love is the giving out of that within self." (262-44) A dominant theme with the added qualifications that we give to others the best, the most creative that is within us, and we expect nothing in return—unconditional love.

- "[Love] is the willingness to sacrifice all of self, even the abilities of self, that others may know the Lord better." (3954-1) A reminder of our responsibility for the spiritual welfare of others—not through preaching or proselytizing, but by demonstrating the expression of love in our own lives.

• Responding to questions about a marriage, Cayce replies: "Remember, the union of body, mind and spirit in such as marriage should ever be not for the desire of self but as *one*. Love grows; love endures; love forgiveth; love understands; love keeps those things rather as opportunities that to others would become hardships." (939-1) A recognition of the challenges and opportunities to be encountered in a love relationship.

• We learn what love is also by understanding what it is *not:* "If even filial or marital or soul love seeks the exalting of self, then it is not fulfilling its purpose from the spiritual import. God is love! The influence or force that motivates the life of each soul is love! But it may be love of self, of fame, of fortune, of glory, of beauty, or of self-indulgence, self-aggrandizement, or the satisfaction to the ego!" (1579-1) Cayce also points out in other readings that love is not simply affection or a physical passion, it is incompatible with fear; it does not coexist with negative or destructive thoughts; and it is not possessive.

• "If ye would have love, show thyself lovely; not only to those that speak kindly to thee . . . " (262-83) Two fundamental ideas here, recurring frequently in the readings: Love is experienced when you, yourself, express it in your life, not when you wait for it to be poured out to you by others. And you should love without discriminating between those who look favorably on you and those who do not.

Against this mind-stretching abundance of ideas about

love, we will focus on the question of how to select a partner for a long-term love relationship.

Choosing a Marriage Partner

If a relationship is to bring us closer to our purpose in life and allow us to experience love in the fruitful ways expressed above, the choice of a marriage partner is a crucial one. Several of the Edgar Cayce readings stress the importance of each partner being an effective complement to the other; that is, someone who can help you accomplish the most in life by supporting your use of your best abilities and talents. Such passages indicate that certain relationships are spiritually right in that they help both partners offer the most loving service to God as well as to humankind.

As stated earlier, you do not meet anyone by chance. Each encounter is an opportunity for you to work with your personal ideals. Among those you meet may be several who would be good marriage partners for you. Choosing among them with the purpose of building a love relationship with one of them should include the exploration of their spiritual awareness, their understanding of their spiritual purposes, and their ideals, whether they are acknowledged or not. In another reading, Cayce suggests cultivating friends who strengthen you in your ideals—not those who draw upon your weaknesses and faults.

In a reading advising about marriage, Cayce stated: "There should be sought as to whether the relationships between those of opposite sex are for a united, cooperative service to a living God and of a spiritual prompting, or are they prompted by material desires? If they are prompted by that which has so oft been true—as of convenience, or for only the beauty of the body or of the companionship physical—these must become palls one upon the other. Then the standard would be as He hath given: There must be the *an-*

swering within each that their *spiritual* and *mental* desires are *one!*" (1173-11)

Guidelines for the Marriage Relationship

A twenty-three-year-old woman who had had nineteen previous readings, including readings about her past lives, came to Edgar Cayce seeking advice about her impending marriage (480-20). The text of that reading provides a remarkable series of ideas and suggestions about love relationships. The principal points:

- The partners should each take advantage in their marriage experience of opportunities for their separate and mutual soul growth, as well as the development of their wills and other mental qualities.
- Keep in mind that a marriage "is to be a fifty-fifty proposition, with you each supplying that which is best within yourselves."
- Be considerate of one another.
- Be cooperative with one another.
- Be interested in one another's activities as though they were your own, and yet each of you should live your own life, have your own interests and your own responsibilities.
- Budget time for the relationship, including for joint social and recreational activities.
- Allow time for rejuvenation when necessary. When challenges and difficulties arise in the relationship, reason together instead of reacting with anger or resentment.
- Meditate and pray together, especially for guidance in the resolution of "doubts and fears and troubles [that] arise (as they must, as they will in the experience of all) . . . "

- Let your attitudes and actions be directed by the spirit of helpfulness and hopefulness.
- Sow "the seeds of truth, of hope" that they may nurture the relationship and "grow into that garden of beauty that makes indeed for the home."

In other readings on love relationships, Edgar Cayce included the following additional ideas:

- Choose your attitudes and actions in accord with your personal ideals.
- Demonstrate in your own attitudes and actions those qualities you are seeking in your partner.
- Correct your negative or judgmental attitudes, and right action is likely to follow.
- Minimize your perceptions of faults, and maximize the virtues.
- Find where you agree instead of where you disagree.
- Do not be possessive of one another.
- Be forgiving of one another and of self.
- Be willing to subjugate your ego, your "I am," your own interests and freedoms to a united effort.
- Remember that the first place to look for changes to improve a relationship is within yourself.
- Acknowledge the possible influence of past-life relationships and karmic effects.

Because of the uniqueness of the Edgar Cayce material on past-life effects on relationships, the remainder of this chapter is devoted to discussion of this material, primarily through the presentation of cases explored in the readings themselves.

The Influence of Past Lives
on Today's Love Relationships

The Edgar Cayce readings often suggested that the potential for growth in many relationships is influenced by patterns created during previous incarnations. I believe we are all under such influences and need to watch for them and take advantage of the opportunities they hold for us. If we examine our love relationships today using the theory of reincarnation as a working hypothesis, we may be able to identify and build upon the positive patterns being carried over within the relationships.

I believe I watched such a relationship between my parents, both of whom had received many readings from Edgar Cayce. The readings indicated that, during an earlier lifetime together, they had created a pattern of helping each other. The readings suggested many times that they build upon this pattern by working together to help each other develop their strengths and achieve a sense of personal fulfillment. Over the years, my brother and I saw them do this repeatedly with one another. Both of them felt that two people don't have to like the same things, but each must want for the other what that person wants for himself or herself.

Their readings also pointed out several other patterns from the past for them to work on. One was the ability to identify aspects of the partner that need support or shoring up, and to answer that need with an interest or strength in oneself. For example, my mother put a lot of positive energy into creating a secure home environment for our family, which proved to be a source of strength and stability for my father. And my father enabled my mother to reach out beyond the home by providing her with opportunities to travel and establish contacts with a variety of people. These activities were suggested by their readings as ways of giving one another support.

A third pattern my parents were able to build upon was a mutual trust which, according to their readings, had been created during previous lifetimes. This enabled each of them to serve as a sounding board for the other regarding life's decisions. My mom's ability to listen and reflect, for example, often greatly helped my dad in decisions related to his work.

An important issue that emerged from my parents' readings is that, as they each clarified their ideals—particularly their ideals related to service—they could see more clearly how they could support one another and love each other more deeply. This clarification of ideals is another pattern that had been built in past lifetimes and was awakened in this one.

The potential helpfulness of patterns built in past lives is clearly demonstrated in the cases of people who were told in their Cayce readings that they could most likely choose not to be reborn into the earth again once their current lives were over. Violet Shelley reported her interesting study of eighteen such people in her book, *Reincarnation Unnecessary*. She attempted to identify patterns at work that would help us understand what would make it unnecessary to reincarnate again.

As I reviewed the lives and readings of these people—some of whom I knew quite well—several patterns emerged. These include: a continuing effort to clarify an ideal and work toward it from lifetime to lifetime; focusing on service as part of one's life; putting aside self and the ego; expressing the fruits of the spirit; and strengthening the will and the ability to make choices in accord with one's values and ideals.

None of these eighteen people was a saint or someone we would typically define as perfect. Yet, by building positive attributes from lifetime to lifetime, by learning throughout the past to understand and practice love, each of these souls had moved to the point where it could choose not to reincarnate in the earth again.

Love relationships provide not only a chance for us to capitalize on positive patterns from the past, they also give us opportunities to overcome problems we've created in the past. The fresh perspective of a relationship in this life may provide the stimulus to take corrective action or to tackle the problem and move through it. Even the pain we feel in a current relationship can be a powerful motivation to change the situation. Kahlil Gibran writes in *The Prophet*, "Your pain is the breaking of the shell that encloses your understanding."

We should bear in mind a key concept from the readings when we work with reincarnation in relationships: Our past-life patterns—our karma—does not exist *between people*. Karma is the memory carried by the nonphysical aspects of each *individual* human being from lifetime to lifetime, a part of each soul's record of its own past choices. In confronting past-life patterns, the individual is simply "meeting itself"—experiencing the effects of its own actions taken in previous incarnations.

An analogy I have found helpful in understanding and using the concept of karma is that it's a little like our relationship with food and eating: It's not that any specific food is for us or against us, but there are lawful consequences of what we choose to eat. To say that a particular food hurts us or that some other food helps us is a distortion. We are not accountable for the nature of various foods; but we are responsible for our own individual choice-making process. Relationships provide similar opportunities for making choices, and similarly lawful consequences take place as a result of those choices.

A fascinating illustration of how relationships can give us a chance to meet past-life patterns in a positive way is found in the readings and correspondence of a forty-one-year-old

New York woman. People who knew her described her as beautiful, striking, and vivacious. After eighteen years of marriage to a very successful businessman during which they were a part of the important social circles of New York, the woman sought advice from Edgar Cayce.

Her relationship with her husband had been quite difficult for her because he had been sexually impotent through their marriage. The woman, who described herself as an affectionate, emotionally expressive person with lots of energy found the situation frustrating emotionally and physically. Although she had considered divorce several times, her deep love for her husband and her desire not to hurt him kept her in the marriage.

Early in their wedded life, she had had relationships with other men—not, she said, out of a desire to be promiscuous or unfaithful, but because of deep physical and emotional needs not being fulfilled by her husband. These relationships were not continued in recent years due in part, she felt, to her learning to sublimate her energies through spiritual practices such as meditation. With time, her need for sexual expression with her husband had become less crucial, and their relationship had become deeper and more loving. She felt they were both growing in important ways.

This request for a reading was occasioned by the reentry into her life of a man who had known and loved her long before her marriage and with whom she was intimate early in her marriage. The man, married during the earlier relationship and still married to someone this woman knew and liked, now wished to resume a relationship that would include sexual activity. The woman was struggling over whether or not to reestablish an association with him, feeling that it might be helpful to him. She was fairly certain that her husband would not find out. Her correspondence with Edgar Cayce described their earlier relationship and includes the comment: "Peculiar circumstances all along, which spelled karma to me, seemed to have dogged our three lives." (2329-1 correspondence) She asked about the past-life patterns with both her husband and her former lover and sought advice on whether or not to resume a relationship with the lover.

The resulting reading described a past life in France in which she had been married to the man who is now her husband. When he left his wife for several years to fight in the Crusades, he forced his wife to wear a chastity belt—"a stay that prevented . . . liaison with others." (2329-1) The deep resentment she developed toward her husband then developed into a pattern of resentment influencing her in subsequent lifetimes. She was determined "to sometime, somewhere, be free and to 'get even' . . . these have and do become portions of the entity's experience, then, is only the meeting of self." (2329-1)

Now view their relationship in this century in the light of that earlier experience in France: He has a beautiful, desirable wife, but is unable to have a sexually fulfilling relationship with her. She has opportunities to "get even" by having affairs that would probably hurt him; she also has the opportunity to meet the past-life pattern of anger and resentment. She chose to do the latter, deciding not to resume the relationship with the lover—partly because she didn't want to hurt the lover's wife and partly because she had largely moved past her desire to get even. Instead, she chose to build on the positive aspects of her eighteen years of marriage, putting aside her physical desire and any wish to hurt others, adopting in their place patterns of love, kindness, loyalty, and devotion. The readings suggest that, with this choice—exercising her will in accord with her ideals—she had used her past-life patterns to meet herself and grow spiritually.

The story fascinates me because of the woman's choice to overcome her own pattern of resentment and desire to get even. Her husband probably would not have known about it, so it was not something she had to work out with him, but something she had to meet within herself. This demonstrates that karma does not exist *between* individuals, but only *within individuals*. It also demonstrates that, although karma is individual, sometimes each soul's meeting of itself will be played out in relation to another individual known from the past. As noted earlier, souls that were together in past lives often reincarnate at a time when they may be together again.

Encouraging us to accept responsibility for our own situation and our relationships with others is one way the theory of reincarnation can be most helpful. In fact, this criterion of helpfulness is of paramount importance in our discovering and using past-life information. According to the Cayce readings, the key question is not whether reincarnation is a fact or a fiction, but whether or not knowledge of our previous lives is practical and applicable in our lives today. As a reading informed one person, " . . . to find that ye only lived, died and were buried under the cherry tree in Grandmother's garden does not make thee one whit better neighbor, citizen, mother or father! But to know that ye spoke unkindly and suffered for it, and in the present may correct it by being righteous—*that* is worthwhile!" (5753-2)

Indeed, from the perspective of the Cayce material, helping us meet the objectives of spiritual growth is the most suitable purpose not just for our use of past-life information, but for all our activities and experiences in life.

Perhaps the most significant experiences with potential for our growth occur in our love relationships. Several couples who recognized this potential sought readings from Edgar Cayce on how to live and work together successfully, so that their relationship would help them fulfill their life's purpose. The central theme of his responses is the importance of establishing unity of ideals and purposes.

For example, each should strive to help the other make the best possible use of his or her abilities. In this way, two people can "bring one another closer, closer to that spirit of truth, of love, of life ... " (341-48) Thus each becomes a primary source of assistance and support in the other one's spiritual growth, and together they progress toward what could well be the most important goal of any love relationship—moving toward their places as companions and co-creators with God.

Part II

Principles and Issues
in Love Relationships

— Leslie Goodman Cayce —

3

Ideals for the Relationship

*B*efore Charles Thomas and I got married, we talked quite a bit about our ideals. We have continued to do so periodically ever since. Initially, it may have been a shared youthful idealism. Now it is because we recognize that by identifying our individual and joint ideals, we are better able to shape the nature of our relationship. That has helped us a great deal in making adjustments to bridge the considerable differences in our backgrounds and to face ongoing challenges in life.

We met when I was a college student and Charles Thomas, who is ten years older, was lecturing around the country for the A.R.E. on the subject of meditation. I was taking an independent study course on mysticism at the time, which led to my attending a five-day conference on meditation at Unity Village, Missouri. I'd never heard of the sponsoring organization, the Association for Research and Enlightenment, nor its founder, Edgar Cayce, before then. But during that conference I got acquainted not only with the organization's philosophy but was most impressed by one of the conference speakers, Charles Thomas Cayce. Coincidentally, if there are such things in relationships, he was scheduled to lecture for two days at my school, Carlton College in Minnesota, following the meditation conference. This afforded us an opportunity to become better acquainted. We shared ideas with an ease that I had not experienced before. Four months later I signed on for a month-long trip to Egypt and Israel, sponsored by the A.R.E. and led by Charles Thomas. He had traveled extensively before this, for he had been teaching in Europe for several years.

Before we met, Charles Thomas had spent time questioning and quietly testing the validity of the Edgar Cayce concepts. This period extended through graduate school and into his work teaching for the University of Maryland and working for the State Department overseas. Not long before we met, he had agreed to work with his father, Hugh Lynn Cayce, who was then president of the A.R.E.

Soon after we met, I learned of Charles Thomas's ambivalence about marriage or at least a struggle with finding the right partner.

Questions that he posed during this time of getting acquainted intrigued me, such as, "Where would you like to be in five years?" These were questions I hadn't been asked before. Though I didn't know it, they were about ideals. They inspired some very candid dialogue and honest searching. We found that we were—and remain—attracted to the honesty in the other.

During the years after we met, because I was still in school, we were apart about half the time. For two years after I graduated we were together, and I then felt clear and ready for marriage but wondered whether it would happen because of Charles Thomas's ambivalence. It was even more clear to me that I not push him into it. His indecision focused on the issue of whether or not he was to marry. Two years later, after extended dialogues and prayers, he felt his indecision melt away. We were married within two months.

We have lived all our married life on a ten-acre farm on the outskirts of Virginia Beach. In a way this fulfills an ideal that we shared. Charles Thomas grew up living a few blocks from the ocean in Virginia Beach, but spent many summers as a child on his uncle's big tobacco farm in North Carolina. He always loved it there. I grew up in a suburb of New York and, during one important year as a teenager, I made several lifelong "decisions" or ideals. One was that I wanted to live on a farm. Our farm was bought by Charles Thomas before we met, and when I first set foot on it I felt an immediate affinity. It fit.

Not long after we were married in 1977, when Charles Thomas was serving as director of Youth Activities at the A.R.E., his father suffered a heart attack that forced him to reduce his heavy work schedule as the leader of the A.R.E. Hugh Lynn moved to chairman of the Board of Trustees, and the board offered Charles Thomas the position of president. This was a major and hard decision for Charles Thomas, who questioned whether his own quiet temperament was best suited to this leadership position. He accepted the job, however, and the challenges began immediately and have never stopped.

I completed my graduate work in social work after our wedding and worked as a social worker for a year before delivering our first child, Corinne. We agreed before our marriage, when we shared our goals and ideals—that while

our children were very young—I would remain at home
with them. Quitting my job didn't feel like a loss or a sacrifice to me, for the gain in my personal life was immeasur-
able. It was a reflection of our deeper ideals related to
children and service. Two years later our second child,
Catherine, was born, and I devoted my undivided attention
to motherhood for four-and-a-half more years. Assuredly,
it wasn't easy being a full-time mother because of all the
innumerable subtle challenges of parenthood. Yet I sometimes think that it was during this period that I really began
to grow up.

Many years later after I returned to work, I reaffirmed our
commitment to family as a top priority by choosing to remain part time when my employer offered me a full-time
position. It was a risky decision because I loved the job and
didn't want to lose it. More important, though, I didn't want
to lose the precious time with our children (then ages eight
and ten) which part-time working affords me. It was another decision in harmony with our ideals. It illustrates, also,
how important ideals are in helping us chart the direction
of our lives.

How to Do It. When Charles Thomas and I first began
talking about our ideals for our relationship, I had the same
initial response I have today—over seventeen years later
when we periodically review and revise them; I feel excitement and anticipation! This is because for me, above all,
setting ideals is a handle; it is a way of having some control
over this most central relationship. It is a way of clarifying
priorities: identifying what is important to me and to us,
seeing where we converge and where we separate, seeing
where we are and where we'd like to be headed. Most of all,
I feel excited because we are making creative choices and
setting directions and courses—being proactive as opposed
to reacting to circumstances. I feel more centered because
of working with ideals. And within our relationship, work-

ing with ideals helps me understand Charles Thomas better, for if you can see more clearly what is important to someone else, it is a step toward clarifying what makes that person tick.

As defined by the Edgar Cayce readings, setting ideals is like pointing oneself in the direction one would like to be headed. They are broad, basic, forming the foundation upon which to stand and meet the world.

More specifically, ideals are divided into three categories: spiritual, mental, and physical. The Edgar Cayce readings suggested using three columns or circles when setting ideals, and we have, so far, always done this. We begin with the spiritual because it sets the tone for all else that follows. Here's an example of an ideals sheet of ours done at the time of our marriage:

SPIRITUAL

Being with God top priority

To know God and Jesus better

MENTAL

Think of "us" before "me"

Openess with each other

More open about inner self

Unattached to farm

Acceptance, uncritical, nondefensive with each other

Keeping the spark alive

Nurture each other's strengths

Keep sense of humor about each other and life

Simplicity

Stimulate each other intellectually

PHYSICAL

Meditate and pray together daily

Sharing/verbalizing our feelings when happy and irritated; put others first

Share dreams and sensitive areas; risking; following through with intuitive feelings

Model farm and open home

Be truthful with each other about little things

Do new, fun things together

Keep doing things that we both love:
    canoeing
    sailing
    dinners by fire
    trips

Encourage, reinforce, help create situations where they can be used

Encourage CT and children

Encourage L's writing and music

Spiritual disciplines:
    Search for God Study Group
    Small group work

The spiritual words are more like one-word triggers to remind us of our philosophy. Affirmations are also statements of spiritual ideals, such as "Lord, here am I—use me in the way *Thou* seest that I may be the greater channel of blessings to those I meet day by day." (1599-1)

The mental ideals are the attitudes or qualities we seek to nurture and to see grow over time. It is here that it becomes clearer how individual ideals can diverge from those of a couple. The focus shifts. Individually, I may focus on an attitude, such as assertiveness, in my work; yet as a couple the focus or statement of an ideal could easily be receptivity and gentleness.

In the physical area, we ask ourselves: How do we want to spend our time? What's important? What makes me feel enlivened and enriched? Again, it is quickly seen how the answers may vary for an individual or a couple. It is interesting now to look back at our ideals sheet from when we first married compared to the most recent one (usually we revise it around the first of the year). We think we have changed so much (and in ways we have), yet basically our ideals remain the same! Ideals are defined as what we strive toward. They seem to embody our central values. Looked at this way, it does make sense that they haven't changed a great deal over the years. For example, it is still so central to us to have an ongoing, active, personal relationship to God (a spiritual ideal); to support and strengthen that through regular meditation times (physical ideal); to watch, even police our emotions and reactions as barometers to where we are at a given time (mental).

Potential Problems or Challenges. A tricky yet interesting aspect of working on ideals with a partner about your relationship is this: Once ideals have been mutually agreed upon—such as, in our case, the primary importance of a spiritual life—it seems wise then to hold yourself responsible for *your* part only. Charles Thomas likes to say there are two main paths to God—one through meditation, the other by the "scruff of the neck." By that he means the route of choosing responses moment by moment that align with the fruits of the spirit (love, attunement, patience, forgiveness, long-suffering, compassion). In these actual moments of choosing, it can really feel like picking oneself up by the scruff of the neck—away from a negative, habitual response and toward a more positive and loving response. I may go through life learning and working on ideals more outwardly—"scruff of the neck" learning. He may be more reflective, meditative, solitary. Who's to say who's working "more" or harder? Yet there is the temptation to compare. I shouldn't try to chart or even follow his course, nor he mine.

We all battle the tendency to pass judgment on others, particularly those closest to us. There is no exception when working and living with ideals with a partner: "Is he/she pulling his/her weight?" "I am working harder/doing better." In our case, there's the temptation to equate frequency of meditation with greater movement toward our spiritual ideal. When we succumb to the temptation to misuse the ideals process in that way, we are defeating a primary purpose—that of working together toward common goals. Instead, we become competitive and judgmental, overseeing another's progress instead of simply focusing on our own. Ideals do not necessarily move us away from our personalities or age-old patterns. So far, my path to God is predominately the "scruff of the neck" route; Charles Thomas's way is more through regular meditation. We are each tempted to pass judgment—on each other, on ourselves—on which path is better. The more *aware* we are of that temptation, the less we fall prey to it.

The Process

The actual process of setting ideals must, by definition, be individualistic. There are no rights and wrongs, do's and don'ts. It can take one person/couple an hour, or another several weeks. It can be done separately first, or the couple may do it together the entire time. I watch for and discard superfluous "shoulds" about the correct way to set ideals. Charles Thomas and I had each worked with ideals before we tried setting them together. While that seemed to help, there is a distinct difference between ideals set for oneself and ideals set with a partner for a relationship. Each time we do it, we must trust ourselves and each other as ideals emerge. Put another way: we are never on the wrong track.

When we focus on our ideals, there are several byproducts that I find insightful. I like to watch the dynamics: How are we relating to each other during it all? As we brainstorm different ideals, it's more interesting if I can stand back and watch our reactions. When Charles Thomas suggests one and I resist, I wonder whether it is because of the process (he's taking over; or it's his turn; will he be offended if I reject that one? I *should* agree) or because of the content (I "should" like that thought, but do I really?!). Truly *honest* work with ideals will automatically hit on some sensitive areas calling for deep, open sharing. With the example just given, I have a choice: to reveal and share my resistance—a step toward deeper sharing—or to conceal it so as not to rock the boat. That choice is present at every step, and I see it as just as important as the actual ideals-setting. Choosing to share one's inner reactions *during* the process often feels scary (because we're more vulnerable), yet that deeper sharing is what can make it so vital, challenging, and exciting.

A sensitive area between Charles Thomas and me has concerned being alone/separate from each other versus being together. It is the tension between self and the couple. We answer to different calls. In addition to work and being with Charles Thomas and the children, I answer to a strong call for time alone and time spent with close friends. Charles Thomas devotes himself more solely to his work and his homelife (family and work on the farm).

Initially, I felt I "should" be more devoted to work, children, and our marriage in a way *similar to* his. I downplayed my attraction to spending time alone and with friends. Our ideals during these times reflected my reticence; my voice as an equal, active partner was still wavering and unsure. Now I see each of us changing, see some of our "shoulds" slip away. I am no longer as apologetic about my needs and

interests, and Charles Thomas is more accepting of that part
of me. Charles Thomas and I see such growth as an example
of Fromm's thesis: that mature love involves preserving
one's individuality.

Another byproduct of sharing our ideals is that we continue to learn more about each other as individuals. As a
couple, of course, we see where and how we've changed
over the years, yet I always enjoy getting new glimpses into
this individual I've been with for over twenty years. Specifically a recent glimpse has revealed a person with real flexibility, while being solid as a rock—true to his convictions. It
seems to me sad for a close relationship if the sense of mystery (who really *is* that person?) and the excitement of discovery has disappeared. Working on ideals together fosters
and nurtures that excitement. (So, we discovered, does writing a book together!)

Working on ideals touches on important dimensions of
our relationship that we discuss in the process. Some of the
more significant ones to me were:

- *Commitment.*   How is it defined? Where do we
stand? How important is it (i.e., committed to another's
spiritual growth and/or committed to the life of the relationship)? "Through thick and thin"—do we buy into it?
How so? When personal growth seems to stray from the relationship, what then?
- *Separation.*   Time alone vs. time together—how
much of each do we each need? Do we accept the differences?
- *Balance.*   How do we each define it? I feel more balanced with time given to friendships and solitude. Charles
Thomas may not. For him to feel things are balanced, time
spent in meditation, prayer, and nature is more critical. A
sense of balance is unique to the individual. How do we
honor and give adequate space for our differences? Is it the
same or different for us?

- *Honesty.* Are we willing to disagree, to hash it out, to give, and to stand firm? Are we sensitive to when defensiveness occurs in each? Where are we guarded, self-protective, and why? Where are we open and candid?

Moving Toward a Oneness of Purpose

I sometimes think that entering in a genuine, authentic, deep way into the process of setting ideals with a partner is akin to embarking on a path of soul (individuation) growth or spiritual development, in this way: At the onset, each individual tries to clarify his/her priorities, goals, values, and action plans. This is followed in the process by a phase of some relinquishing and compromise, further prioritizing, reaching some stalemates, impasses, and—most of all for me—learning to let go. It seems a paradox to clarify what is important and then to be willing to forsake it. But this process, repeatedly over time, can serve as a refinement, a fine tuning of the self: This is who I am, but I can give it up! Clarify and detach an ideal of the ideals process. Here's an example of how it has worked in our marriage:

Over the last year and a half I have been trying to balance certain areas of our marriage that had imperceptibly grown out of whack. I am more prone than I'd like to believe to suppressing my needs and preferences in deference to Charles Thomas's as stated earlier. This has been a sometimes rocky, shaky process; yet it *is* part of our ideals to have an equal marriage, as we continue to define what that means. For me to state a desire that I know Charles Thomas wouldn't understand; i.e., to be with a friend when I could be with him, is still hard, but it used to be much harder. I felt the need to explain, even to justify, my desire to visit a friend. It was as though, if I had a good reason, I might be deserving. This pattern, reminiscent of a parent-child relationship, needed to be replaced with an updated model! Having set a previous ideal of equality within the marriage had the effect of shining a light on the imbalance within that dynamic.

After periodic (and often difficult) discussions sprinkled throughout eighteen months, we have reached more of an equilibrium. This has been a sensitive area for Charles Thomas as well because it touches on the subject of separateness within marriage. His dilemma arises because separateness while remaining open and vulnerable *feels* very scary to him. It has meant conscious choices to step out on faith for him to honestly let loose without withdrawing to protect himself. It continues to be hard. There have been occasions when I was out in the evenings. Upon returning, I could feel his distancing—protecting himself, punishing me. In the past this "worked" for him by making me uncomfortable enough to forsake some outside interests. Now I take note of it with the hope that each time it will grow smoother for us and it really has. I have gotten clear on the importance of *more balance* in this part of our relationship. I don't need to justify. I can explain, but am not so inhibited by his disapproval or lack of understanding. He, meanwhile, grows more accepting and less withdrawn all the time. He trusts me and us more, truly not seeing my friendships as a threat any more.

In this example we set the ideal—equality—long ago. The refining within the implementation of it continues actively day by day. In theory, we are in accord, having jointly set the ideal of equality; in reality, it can take some hard work over time. The implementation phase is still evolving, while the ideal—to be balanced, equal—remains strong and constant.

As we accept each other as we are, there is not only more balance within our relationship, but, like a ripple effect of a stone in the water, more acceptance in all of our relationships.

My intuition is that ultimately I'll be able and willing to *let go* of the need for more balance in the self versus the couple arena. Because this tension had been heavy, in recent years readjustment has been a strong need. It will be a full circle where Charles Thomas and I are each secure, loving, and trusting enough to be able to each relinquish views that may feel crucial individually—for a "bigger purpose." That relinquishing, that detachment from need—clarify and let go—is an ultimate ideal.

There have been glimpses of experiencing that ultimate, as when I have chosen to be with or apart from Charles Thomas without feeling that I was losing ground or regressing. Likewise, he has sometimes genuinely felt fine before and after I went out with friends. In other words, we've each relinquished what felt important, stepping out on faith. Somewhere in the process, we tap into a sense of oneness. It is when that happens that a specific ideal, like acceptance and equality in marriage, becomes the means to this end— oneness. Working on ideals seems to lead to this door. Once there, it doesn't matter who says or does what; we are together in a *deep* sense that encompasses and surpasses. We catch a glimpse, a taste of living our ideals, just enough to know that it is possible! Just enough to whet our appetites, to help us forge ahead, more deeply committed to our work with ideals.

Spiritual Ideals

I am Jewish, Charles Thomas is Protestant. Before our marriage, we were "interviewed" by the rabbi performing the ceremony and asked the inevitable question: "In which religion will you rear your children?" We spoke to him of our belief in God through different religions and our shared spiritual search and disciplines. We said we hoped to share this with our children, exposing them to both religions and helping them decide for themselves. Our response, while undoubtedly inadequate to him, had more to do with spiritual ideals than it did with any particular religion. We spoke to him about our spiritual beliefs in oneness and manifesting fruits of the spirit.

The Cayce readings often seem like a long sermon filled with deep inspiration. They speak as eloquently as any religion's scripture about spiritual ideals that transcend religious differences: To know that the Lord thy God is One (traditional Jewish terminology, but undoubtedly acceptable to all) and to manifest the fruits of the spirit (traditional Christian terms, also acceptable to all)—or to be a channel of blessings today, now to all I contact (again, universally meaningful). Each time I read these statements of spiritual ideals and variations on these themes, I have that sense of "Ah, I've come home." Such simple statements are easy to grasp, to understand, to sink your teeth into, to try to implement. They have a power, a challenge, and an ability to move me that doesn't diminish with time.

Because Charles Thomas and I share not only these ideals but a primary value placed on them, I felt quietly comfortable with the rabbi's question. I felt we had a solid foundation on which to stand and to build. We share a view that sees the life force as good, loving, and purposeful, that sees our task as one of attuning ourselves to that one Spirit. Holding those fundamental views in common, I felt we were strong. I still feel we are fortified, even in the midst of grappling with decisions about our children's religious upbringing, now facing the logistical choices the rabbi was cautioning us about. Yet, because we clarified our spiritual ideals, we have a clear sense of where we stand—where we're coming from.

Spiritual ideals form the undergirding to all other aspects of our lives. Interwoven in the tapestry of experiences shared in the following chapters is an unspoken, invisible, current that is such a big part of our bond with each other. It is our commitment to a spiritual path.

To me, shared spiritual ideals are a bonus, icing on the cake. Individually, spiritual ideals are a necessity for me, a steadying anchor throughout the storm. Ideals also spark unique and creative experiences. I use those words deliberately because I cannot honestly say working with ideals has made life easier or lessened the pain or confusion. Yet I'm not sure that is the purpose. Working with ideals provides a *focus* amidst many sensory and intellectual challenges and distractions. It helps keep me centered, and it offers a sense of personal power as opposed to the deep helplessness so easily evoked by the pull of impersonal forces in today's society.

Through critical periods in a personal relationship and through times of distancing or change of any sort, a return to ideals work is a steadying and decisive effort.

As I study the Cayce readings, spiritual ideals revolve around these thoughts: "Not my will but Thine, O Lord, be done in and through me." "May I respond to or see this situation from the best or highest in me." "May I be a channel of blessings here, now, to those I contact in every way."

These sorts of prayers or affirmations are deceptively simple, universal, and transcendent, integrating institutional religions and ecumenical dogma. While they are spiritual in origin and intent, one can readily grasp them mentally and begin to implement them outwardly or physically. I am indebted to the readings for grounding spiritual or metaphysical concepts. "Just a little gentleness or kindness or patience, today" is typical of their message. It is a message easily taken into the heart and easily referred to. Ideals are meant, paradoxically, to be both put away and lived with. We remember, we let go. I ask to be guided—in my actions this day—and then I proceed, putting it out of mind.

When a dear friend recently called on the telephone, needing comfort during a very difficult time, I had one of those rare experiences that clarifies briefly where we are—in this case, where I am in my work with spiritual ideals. "Pray that I be strong and clear," she said. Her request echoed in my mind as a spontaneous statement of an ideal of hers. Insight came as I heard my spontaneous statement in response: "I pray that God be her (my) guide." Having a mental picture of the endless routes and different paths of action and responses we can choose at any given time, I sense and trust that there is a God-given path somewhere and I pray that I be sensitized in that direction.

While the path is still shrouded in mystery, I have these clues: It is not a path that puts self first. It is a path on which we learn how to love, and self-acceptance feels crucial to realizing that objective. We are given headings, but the specifics must spring from within *each* of us. There are guidelines, but no rules.

4

⚉

Communicating in
the Relationship

Charles Thomas and I came from quite different family
backgrounds and we grew up on divergent experiences
with communication. My parents set the tone for my family with regular heated discussions. The question may have
been impersonal, say a political or philosophical issue, or
very personal, but opinions were never withheld. We all had
this attitude: I'm going to tell you what I think, you can do
with it what you will. While this approach to communication has its advantages, it facilitated years of painful conflict
between my father and me. My greatest difficulty in communication in a love relationship was with him. I felt that

he was domineering and critical, and I showed my resentment through cold withdrawal and disdain. After years of trying to intellectualize, analyze, and basically "work it out myself," I turned in despair to the Cayce readings with a deep sense of "I cannot do this alone."

This realization occurred when I was nineteen years old. I had been away at school for three years; yet with each visit home, it was clearer how tied I was to that relationship emotionally. Whenever I came home to visit, I was dismayed by how automatically my father and I fell into our damaging, distancing, painful communication patterns. Truly, I felt caught. While I wanted to change, to alter my reactions, I repeatedly fell into our well-worn pattern/cycle.

While at college I had, through the Cayce readings, come to view relationships as karmic, believing that there is a reason why I feel and behave as I do with another person. And, in difficult situations particularly, there is something to be learned by paying attention to my feelings and responses. When I find it hard or irritating to be with someone, it is immensely helpful to take that as an indication that I am perceiving or projecting a quality that is hard for me to face in myself. Trying to modify my reactions is a concrete way of working on myself, and this to me is what becoming aware of karma entails. By accepting the idea of karma, we take responsibility for our attitudes. My painful relationship with my father has taught me the meaning of karma, and from this experience I've learned of the ever-present potential for changing difficult relationships.

It was because this philosophy had grown so strong that I couldn't sit comfortably with my miserable relationship with my father which was not getting any easier or smoother. Each time I came home for a visit we fell into the patterns of interaction that had grown up between us over many years, old worn patterns that were built on my resentments and hurts from the power he had over me and his frustrations with my not conforming to or being what he wanted. As we became more defensive with each other, it became harder and harder for us to communicate. Finally I had to stand back from this picture to try to understand the overall tone of the feelings that had grown up between us. I began to see clearly that the negative feelings were part of a larger pattern, a way of relating to each other, that we had created. Each incident, each conflict was not separate from other difficulties we had; they were interrelated. Old responses of resentment and resistance rose in me almost of their own accord. How hard it was to look at the ugly parts of myself that dominated the relationship.

My reaction to Dad had become so guarded that all my feelings of love were squelched. I searched for genuine positive feelings—feeling guilty that I had to search and, in the process, watched myself turn away from my father and hurt him. This pattern had become so familiar, so easy to fall into that I frequently felt like a victim of conditioned responses. Because our ingrained attitudes meant hurting each other, they were harder and harder for me to reconcile. Even though I had been "trying" for years to improve our relationship by writing letters while in college and confronting my father, without much success, I was as caught up in it as ever. I couldn't convince myself by saying, "I'd done all I could." I knew that I hadn't.

I had resisted giving of myself to my father in any way—giving him my attention and interest; giving him authority over me; giving him love and tenderness. Until I had at least tried to give to him in some way, I knew I hadn't done all that I could.

The conflicts in my relationship with my father served to accentuate my limitations. Frequently I heard myself say, "I will not and cannot 'give' in this way. I won't give in to him." When I began to contemplate more seriously the possibility of changing my attitudes, things began to happen. As I saw our interaction as a pattern we both had constructed, I also saw that with each incident there was the choice to continue building the same patterns or to respond differently. Realizing that I could choose to alter my responses was hard because it meant taking responsibility for what happened between us. I could no longer blame my father.

Seeing this relationship as a pattern the two of us had built and owning up to that and seeing it as an opportunity to grow beyond my limitations, I had a new meaning to the concept of karma. Beginning to view the relationship with my father as karmic meant coming to terms with the fact that, sooner or later, I would have to *face what we had built,* I would have to work with it in some way. If I tried to avoid or ignore our conflicts, they would still exist. Growth occurs when we choose to face recurring difficulties, and I could see specific ways in which I would grow by changing my attitudes toward my father.

When I began to see our relationship in this light, I had already realized that Dad wasn't going to change to suit my needs. I also knew that I couldn't force change on myself. My general attitude at that time is conveyed in the following journal entry, written while I was living with my parents and feeling caught in the pattern of this difficult relationship:

"I suppose I blame Dad for not working with himself more, for giving in to himself. His guilty conscience about his own laziness toward self-analysis is projected onto us, his children. It seems as if he, too, dislikes himself for not being more sensitive to others, for not trying more to change.

"He is inconsistent and sets poor examples of the person that he is. He can demand his own way, demand that we do as he says and then demand that we respect him. I cannot give that to him.

"What it amounts to with me is that I don't like him and

can't get beyond that. Now is a time when he wants my love and I cannot give it. I hurt him by my disregard. The primary feeling I have now is regret that I upset and hurt him, that I could not bring myself to sincerely embrace him. It calls for more sacrifice than I can sincerely give. I see I am not ready to forsake all the old deep injuries from the past and to love him *in spite of* the suffering I have known. I cannot yet forgive and forget the little things. I see I am not ready to give of myself in this way."

I would write things like this after emotional scenes that I really didn't understand. Many times I couldn't see where the hostility that arose in us came from. So I would write, letting out the first things that came to mind in the hope that even the dimmest light would be cast on the dynamics between us. I was stumped. I'd reached the limits of my understanding. Each time I came home I was struck with the reality that I didn't like my father and couldn't respond warmly to his attempts to be with me. But I didn't have a clear picture of him at all because so much of what I saw in him were qualities of my own that I disliked. His actions confronted me with the fact that I couldn't accept certain qualities in myself. Blatantly rejecting him meant rejecting the parts of myself that he represented. It also meant hurting him. Watching myself turn away from him went against everything I believed in and yet it was as though I couldn't stop myself. It became harder and harder to continue in the relationship as it was. I saw with increasing clarity that *here was an opportunity to accept myself more and to learn to be receptive* rather than resistant to my father. Most of all I saw it as an opportunity to let go—of the pain and the past. I had a great deal of pride invested in our "old" relationship. Here was the chance to *give it up*. It was a risk. I knew how deeply he had hurt me in the past when I had been more open.

Yet I found that I couldn't force a change in attitude on

myself, though I tried and wanted to. The thoughts I shared
had been germinating for a long time before they reached
my heart and my actions. For over a year I thought about
the relationship in terms of karma, as something I'd helped
to create that had the definite potential for either continued pain or for growth, when I was ready to let go of the
pain. I started to balance out the conscious efforts I'd been
making with an explicit acknowledgment of and faith in the
power of unconscious forces. Although I had lots of hope in
the future of this relationship, I had reached the point where
I felt I'd done all I consciously could and needed help.

I started to pray every day as a way of asking for help. It
was a vehicle for stepping outside of conscious methods
and recognizing that potential of unconscious processes.
My prayers were not specific. I did not understand the feelings in both of us enough to try to predict or decide what
needed to change. Praying was a way of affirming and re-
affirming daily my openness to change. Because I had so
clearly reached a dead end from trying to work on our relationship by myself, I now feel that the daily prayers played a
decisive role in the positive changes that have occurred.

Almost a year after I'd been praying, when I came home
for a visit, it wasn't long before tensions were mounting and
familiar feelings of defensiveness indicated that the old patterns were at work. Only this time I saw clearly, as a typical
scene was about to be enacted, that the choice was mine to
respond differently. Here is what I wrote at the time:

"As Dad fell into an emotional state, provoked by my
usual way of being cold and removed from him, I could see
it all beginning once again. His anger and hostility begins in
the form of verbal abuse and accusations. As always, they
initiate my withdrawal in self-defense. I have taken his abu-
sive manner as an indication of his disapproval and dislike
of me (which makes his displays of love hypocritical). In his
anger he is like a child, demanding acknowledgment of his

authority and power and I could not give him that. It would mean bending under him, it would be weak.

"This weekend as we talked, I felt the old responses begin to dwindle. During the few moments when he went in the house, I was left viewing the start of our old interaction and saw the choice looming distinctly before me: to either remain as I've been all along (unresponsive, resentful) or to tell him that he was right about my rudeness, right to be angry with me.

"When he came back, we walked out in the yard and with my heart pounding, feeling that I was close to sacrificing for the first time, I said it. He probably didn't know how hard it was (for me) to say and mean it for the first time, 'You are right.' I could grant him his emotional outbursts without feeling that if I didn't resist them or fight them, I would crumble under the power of his words and his strength. The outbursts have little meaning; they fall from his lips and his child-emotions, not from his heart. For once, I didn't dwell on them. As I listen to his agreeing with me, that he is right, it seems like a test of my honesty. Waves of the old defensiveness wash over me, anger at his accusations, wanting him to be different. Then they are replaced by a new detachment and a feeling of separateness from him. Suddenly I feel a new space between us. He is entitled to accuse or whatever without it affecting me so much. His accusations do not hurt; they do not take away my dignity; I am still intact.

"The emotional part of Dad is but a small part of him. I have felt so intimately wound up in it, it was all I could see. I take a step or two away from him and get a broader, clearer view. There is a freedom; I can breathe. I have been resisting and doubting my father's love. Now I begin saying to him, 'Yes! Yes, I like you (and you like me).' Touches of giving and forgiving . . . things I haven't known."

Now, many years later, our relationship has radically

changed. At the turning point described in my journal, I felt a release from the rigid patterns of the past. I discovered a receptive side of myself that is stronger than I thought, and I discovered fine qualities in my father. As I've been able to perceive him through a clearer lens, I've seen his fine intelligence and penetrating mind, his instinctive generosity, and—perhaps most poignantly—his continuing attempts to give, to compromise, to accommodate. Finally we share genuine affection. We share a respect and warmth that we didn't know existed when I was younger.

I do not take the "happy ending" quality of this experience lightly, nor do I claim all the credit for the positive changes that transpired. I am awed by its resolution; I am inspired by the hope it contains for transforming other difficult relationships and situations into brighter, more beneficial experiences. As vividly as I can recall the dismal feeling that there is just too much misunderstanding and pain ever to be free from, I cannot help but contrast that with the present ease with which we relate. I now see that need to sort through all of the past conflicts in order to smooth them out. Although I'm sure that the conscious attempts we both made throughout the years contributed to subsequent changes, in the end this process of change, of letting go of deep-rooted attitudes and communication patterns is as mysterious as ever to me. The experience with my father will continue to stand as an example of a "working through of some karma" by seeing ingrained attitudes as old patterns that I have the choice to build or to leave behind.

Over the years since the initial breakthrough in communication with my father, there have been a handful of situations between us that looked and sounded like the "early years," in which our old patterns were being revved up, and it would have been easy and familiar to fall back into them. There was an incident when we did that and ended up yelling at each other, as my children watched. Later, as my father and I talked it over, he accused me of having reverted to all the hostility and resentment of my adolescence. But I knew it wasn't so. My responses this time were different. Where once his observations would have made me defensive, now I considered them and said, "All I feel is regret— no hostility—over the incident." It was icing on the cake that he, in turn, could *hear* that as truth. Yet it was more valuable that I knew it as truth. The patterns of discord still exist between us, but their hold on us has vastly diminished, replaced by far more positive feelings. It was for me an example of being freed of burdensome baggage, lifted out of ego-centered reactions toward responses more in line with my ideals. It feels like grace in action, in which arguments that once held the weight of an unresolved past become clearer, lighter, more focused on the present situation, less muddied by old patterns.

By contrast with my family's confrontational approach, Charles Thomas's family sidestepped conflict, withheld criticism, and valued noninterference. Displays of so-called "negativity" as I was accustomed to were avoided in his family.

As a consequence of our different ways, Charles Thomas has an innate tendency to shy away from emotional exchanges. My father, nonetheless, adores Charles Thomas's characteristically silent attention during such exchanges.

When Charles Thomas met my emotions with silence during our early years together, I couldn't understand it. He was too confused by my behavior to articulate his own feelings. We were both in new territory. Many of the patterns from my childhood didn't suit him, and to reach one another we've almost had to create a new way of communicating.

While marital advisors emphasize the importance of communication, it has to be *effective* communication. A successful relationship, we are told, requires saying what you mean, listening, thus expressing feelings, staying on the subject, and arguing effectively.

While the advice is endless, a realistic and simple goal is to be clear, especially with loved ones. There are a few essential tools that facilitate clarity. Tools often recommended in the Cayce readings include these five:

- Self-observation and striving for detachment;
- Using meditation to calm the mind and all the mental clatter;
- Using the will to choose emotions and responses;
- Making/taking time to listen inwardly and outwardly;
- Watching for patterns (habitual responses, feelings: "He always says/does that." "I always feel . . . when . . . ").

Cultivating Detachment and Self-Observation. This has also been explored extensively by the Russian teacher of mysticism and philosophy, George Gurdjieff. It involves observing one's inner voices, attitudes, and emotions as objectively as possible, in an effort to be free of them. Many of us are usually held in the tight grip of habitual, half-conscious responses. To develop clarity we need to be aware of where we are coming from.

Meditation to Calm the Mind of All the Mental Chatter. Specifically, the readings suggest it as a tool for increasing clarity in decision making and in critical times. It is a natural vehicle for getting to our deeper concerns and tapping the best in us.

Using the Will to Select Our Responses and Emotions. I have already shared a prime example (in my work on the relationship with my father) of using the will to choose a new response. It is a simple phrase, yet one that calls for patience and persistence. It rarely happens overnight.

Making Time to Listen. I have experimented with this tool during some of Charles Thomas's and my most difficult and intense dialogues, times when we are both defensive. The immediate tendency during arguments is to protect and shield oneself by thinking up more and better reasons for being right. The experiment has been to catch myself in the act of defending—either mentally or verbally—and to stop it immediately. I replace defensive tactics with a receptive, open stance of listening, listening without any preconceptions or presumptions of what might be heard next. It is a tool that has proven often to have quite drastic results: turning the tide of an argument away from the isolation of defensive maneuvers toward the oneness of touching the heart.

Keeping on the Alert for Patterns. This is necessary because we are often such automatic response vehicles and don't even know it; it is unconscious. When someone knows how it "pushes our buttons," an important pattern exists. If a red warning light were to go off, indicating an imminent fall into a ditch and the warnings were heeded with a different response, new energy would be tapped. Freedom could be tasted where before it was trapped.

In order to truly and effectively embrace any of these tools, there are a few precursors. Perhaps the most common call to change comes from pain. Being in therapeutic professions, Charles Thomas and I have the experience, supported by research, of repeatedly seeing individuals seek help when they are in crisis. Whatever the cause—from pain to self-growth—a desire to change and to grow is a necessary precursor to initializing such tools. Other important attitudes rest upon oneness: a willingness to relinquish control over people and circumstances, to relinquish defenses or attitudes that may seem so dear, so important. A sense of mystery is another way to view openness. For when there is openness, there is the mystery of reaching an unforeseen outcome. When we let go of tightly held attitudes and emotions, there is the mystery of what lies beyond them.

The Cayce readings, in encouraging couples to talk out

their conflicts, offer specific advice. One woman was told
not to keep her grievances in, but to learn to express them
in loving ways. She was especially encouraged to get her
points across through example rather than preaching. (585-
1) Consistency between words and deeds was stressed as
the chief need of another couple.

Still another couple was advised: "Think not that each
will not find fault one with another; yet, let that mind be in
each to acknowledge error, for each becomes the bigger by
acknowledging, and not committing the same error twice."
They were also told to "Never *rile* for that sake of carrying
points, nor of self-assertion," but to be supportive, bringing
out the best in one another and to pay attention to "the *little
things* that make the larger life the bigger and the better!"
(903-3)

Because of our different backgrounds, arguing effectively
did not come easily for Charles Thomas and me. During our
early years together I was stunned and confused by Charles
Thomas's silence and prolonged withdrawal following a disagreement. He, in turn, seemed shocked and perplexed by
my emotional outbursts. Over the years, we have gradually
modified our early patterns to find a middle ground where
we can meet. We have used the five tools in our search for a
meeting place. No longer do I get an unspoken message to
go off alone to cry or be angry. I've learned that if I make
myself wait (patience) and don't push for confrontation on
my terms, when I want it, Charles Thomas will approach
and discuss a previously emotional issue. Allowing some
time to elapse also offers us each some clarity and the space
to *listen* far better than in the heat of the moment. It means
neither arguing in the heat of emotions, nor dropping completely the bone of contention, but talking over important
issues and problems after the initial emotions have eased
and when there is enough uninterrupted time to focus
calmly together.

Developing a language and a pathway that is mutually acceptable for resolving arguments is a way of nurturing and taking care of a committed relationship. It is taking the offense, if you will, instead of breaking into arguments and being totally thrown off track by them.

Now as I listen to our children bickering, arguing, I am reassured by the reminder that arguments are natural and inevitable. Yet my finer sensibilities object, feeling that we "shouldn't" fight or we "should" place limits where a degree of fighting is permissible but beyond which "something is wrong." As parents, we are usually inclined to impulsively intrude upon our children's arguments to short-circuit or prevent them. Likewise, as a couple, we have the same first instinct. It is an unrealistic assumption that we all share an ability to discern petty irritations due to fatigue, from genuine disagreements over real issues. Children confuse and merge the two. Often, adults do as well. The point, however, is that disagreements are inevitable in committed, intimate relationships.

Accepting, instead of avoiding, this fact was a turning point for us as a couple and as parents. It was a necessary precursor to developing our way of dealing with arguments. It is an interesting aside that our two children seem to mirror our two different backgrounds. One will easily capitulate and give in to avoid disagreement. Her motto seems to be: peace, above all—akin to her father's preference. The other child seems to almost enjoy verbal banter. Making and proving her point would be more her theme—similar to my tendency and many of those in my family of origin.

Once I became less subjective and enmeshed in the details and causes of each altercation and instead began identifying patterns in my and Charles Thomas's approach to conflicts, new light shone on this area.

Our children's presence over the past fourteen years has truly helped clarify the whole area of arguments and their resolution. More often now I see beneath the details or the outer trimmings of a disagreement to a central theme. The "heat" of the argument is in the dynamics—in self-defense, each one feels threatened and heatedly tries to protect her territory, her stance. There is pain or there is the threat of being hurt. Defenses up, we protect. The conflict gains momentum. Resolution, on the other hand, begins to enter in as defenses soften. When we are no longer as afraid, threatened, and/or hurt, the energy moves from the adrenals or stomach up toward the heart. I can sometimes sense this flow in the children, sometimes in myself. Arguments are usually softer with children, and more frequent, and more pertinent. They are clearer, less clouded by patterns of the past. I can see their faces tire of the self-defense mode. That, it seems, is when the energy moves toward the heart. They reach out, they share, they respond to a hug. Children model forgiveness. If they hold a grudge at all, it doesn't seem to last very long. I am trying to reclaim that openness to relinquishing the shield of self-defense (ASAP!). To do that can feel scary, risky; we are no longer defending our position. We are open to attack. Yet, the Cayce readings, the Bible, and the wisdom of sages urge us time and again to forgive. It is a fruit of the spirit. It is basic, timeless, forever relevant, appropriate. And forever a stretch! It pushes us where we are most vulnerable.

When I was on the verge of forgiving my father, moving from self-defense to receptivity/heart, it felt like jumping off a high cliff. I might die, he might trample me emotionally. It's impossible to hold the shield of self-defense and to forgive. Forgiveness means being open. The energy of compassion is so close to love, to the heart. It is a paradox that instead of dying or being hurt when we forgive, we become more alive, expanded, bigger, deeper. We grow when we take the risk and jump.

Arguments and conflicts appear to be vehicles for learning forgiveness. Again, children have helped me see the value of both feeling the anger and the value of letting it go. They do not block or stop the process. They go right along on it. By observing children, I see that learning forgiveness doesn't mean denying the anger or pain or any of the classically termed "negative" emotions; rather, it is trusting and learning to go with a more thorough process, not to get stuck!

When a disagreement pops up, it feels different from the very start when it is entered into with an eye toward forgiveness, as opposed to plunging in to convince another that "I am right." Totally different. In the throes of the self-defense or justification mode, it is usually hard to listen. Remember the "theme song" idea at the start of this chapter? Self-defense is stuck in self; forgiveness and empathy emerge when there is a letting go.

Not that forgiveness comes easy! Rising to an occasion to express or defend myself has, historically, come easier. I am not naturally a patient person and am fairly quick to anger. Furthermore, I can commiserate with one of our children who has such a hard time moving out of expressing her view (self-justification and defense) and into letting go. I encourage her (and myself) with "Say it's OK." As many of us know all too well, it is hard to let go, hard for a child, harder for adults who have been going at it longer. Hard to choose vulnerability.

A reason we chose to emphasize forgiveness as an essential ingredient here is because it seems too often overlooked in marital advice that teaches good communication skills and techniques for "conflict resolution." While it is not our intention to underestimate the value of such skills, we would rather like to add the underrated, powerful effects of heart-centered forgiveness.

A further complication in the life of a love relationship is the see-saw effect. It involves the balancing and integrating of self and the dyad: me/we. There is a continuous volley between opening up, letting go, and remaining true to oneself.

Often this see-saw action lies submerged beneath discussions and arguments. The specific details are more like a cover or foil for more central basic issues, like: Does this mean you still don't love me? How important am I? Did you intend to hurt me? Do you care that I'm hurt? If reassurance is given/felt to these deeper questions, arguments often lose much of their steam.

Sometimes a disagreement ensues because my ego feels threatened, defensive, needing to assert and stake out my boundaries. Other times what appears to be an argument is more a misunderstanding, a difference in perception, uncluttered with ego fears and claims. Usually, there is some of both at play and the search for clarity is on!

I experience the see-saw of self versus the dyad in the tendency to blame myself when disagreements occur. A recent example happened during a rare three-day weekend at home. We had only one social commitment to interrupt the wonderful prospect of time to be together as a family. The first two days unfolded in a dream-like fashion. We had good times working and playing around the farm and at the beach and some unexpected time for the two of us to be alone together, which we welcomed. We entered day number three feeling close, warm, happy. Day three included our one commitment: a friend's afternoon beach party. The children and I went on ahead so that Charles Thomas could do some work before joining us later. When he arrived, I was about to set off with several friends on a long beach walk, which I'd anticipated for hours. As I left for my walk, he went for a dip in the ocean. When I returned sometime later, he'd gone home.

As I drove home, sensing something gone awry, I recognized a familiar pattern at work once again: After that time of closeness and intimacy, I blamed myself for breaking our connection. I interpreted my choice to walk rather than stay with the family as a choice for self.

My habitual response has been to berate myself for "making another mistake." In this instance, there were potentially two mistakes: taking the walk, knowing that Charles Thomas would rather be with me than the other guests; and not telling him where I was going, thereby avoiding facing his need to be with me.

The recurring dilemma is that sometimes my needs vary from his, pulling me in two directions at once. A move in either direction seems somehow to fall short: If I submerge my individual expression (to walk), I feel resentful because I've betrayed myself. Should I choose to walk, I have betrayed and abandoned my family. It seemed like a no-win choice.

My unconscious tendency for a long time was to see personal differences as bad things to be obliterated. That may be irrational and unrealistic. More salient, however, is to simply acknowledge and accept this tendency of mine. I am learning to replace the old word *mistake* and all of its self-condemning connotations, with the word *differences*—differences in our personalities and our reactions. The result was beneficial. An entirely new emotional process is triggered in me. That new process feels far more healthy outside of the dichotomy of good/bad, me/he, or me/we. It flows in the direction of reconciliation and integration.

Consequently, when Charles Thomas and I later discussed the beach incident, I began by feeling less apologetic and self-condemning. This is progress! Often in such situations he does indeed feel that I've made a mistake and asks, "How could you have done that?" which reinforces my habitual pattern of self-condemnation. But I've begun speaking about our differences being all right. Theoretically, of course, apart from an emotional, personal incident, he

knows this. We both do. But we also know that one's most
intimate relationships circumvent the intellect and, by trig-
gering our emotions, show us where we live!

During our post-mortem, I told him that my interest in
taking a walk, in getting exercise, did not reflect any lack of
desire to be with him. We were, in essence, plunged back
into our familiar arena of sensitivity—separateness within
the relationship and trying to feel comfortable with our differences. It was not easy for him to accept my explanation.
In the initial stage, it was laborious and hard, as disagreements often are. I could no longer feel or say, "I'm sorry. I
won't do it again."

He would survive and—it is hoped—learn from that discomfort. I needed to trust my instinct that differences are
all right. I will never be all he wants and needs, never be
able to meet all his needs. I will always *"do something
wrong"*—only now that phrase sounds comical, as if being
myself, an individual with a different set of responses, were
synonymous with doing something wrong! While our differences in this incident might have provoked argument,
with an ensuing period of estrangement, they served as a
stepping-stone to greater understanding and future possibilities.

The resolution of this conflict has been subtle and evolving, unlike the more transparent route when I took the discomfort away in the past. Since that incident he has moved
toward greater acceptance of this personal difference in our
needs, greater trust of separateness. He recognizes this
change. It has been gradual and, probably because of that, I
trust this movement. We have both gained a greater capac-
ity to live with ambiguity or unresolution. Beyond that we
have achieved greater resolution, a new integration for us.
As he has become more accepting of our differences, we are
more open, therefore closer, which is always his desire. It is
an example of the maxim: What you let go of, returns to you.

The intimacy we share is a deeper, more real intimacy between two whole persons, not an accommodation, a compromise of one's or both of our true beings. Along the way, however, it meant, for us, living with greater discomfort at times. This was new for us.

What complicates arguments so often is emotional baggage—in the major form of childhood reactions—unconscious and unresolved—and the accompanying feelings. Most of us don't have the time, energy, and endurance to deal with these forces. Perhaps more common is the relationship in which only one partner has the energy for some introspection. But that is perfectly appropriate since we truly have only ourselves to work with in the first place!

It has been a tremendous source of comfort and reassurance when I have entered the maze of an argument to remember to ask for guidance, to remember that while I have only myself to work with and work on, I need not be alone. I try to be open to the "still, small voice," to hearing God knock upon the door. Conscious acknowledgment of a higher power in and beyond me sets the stage for being lifted out of the more petty, "smaller" ego concerns and for casting off the baggage.

Implicit in the process of personal change is another central thread woven into the fabric of committed relationships. It is that of self-observation, which is closely aligned with detachment. Both are crucial.

Intimate relationships force us or gently call us to look at ourselves closely and not to let up. It is "easy" to choose not to look at oneself, or to avoid being close to another, or when close to place blame outside oneself or make excuses for ourselves like, "That's the way I am." Simple, honest self-observation usually seems to keep in check the tendency to project or place blame elsewhere. Paying attention—another way of phrasing it—is demanding, is work. I have always felt a rush of affinity with a Cayce reading that says, paraphrasing, "Life is work!" It is enthusiastically realistic. It is so true, particularly in love relationships. Powers of discernment, like a muscle, need to be used. With regular use, they grow stronger. When we begin to see and act clearly in the midst of an argument, no doubt compassion is released. When we are in touch with our heart, can "admit" to the fears beneath a defensive argument, transcendence is born and an integration—beyond resolution—brings to our relationships the gift of new life.

5

⚅

The Past Affects the Present

*I*mportant personal relationships define who is in our "molecule." Our molecule includes all of the people around us who are important because of their psychological influence on us. They may be family members, friends, colleagues, employers, children, ex-lovers, spouses, mentors. They may be physically present in our life or part of our past. Anyone who affects us in a deep way emotionally, positively or negatively, is an inhabitant of our molecule. These special people revolve around us, figuratively at least, as we enter into and move through our primary relationships.

I continue to be struck by the influence of many others in my life and upon my relationship with Charles Thomas. It is all too easy to minimize the lasting effect of unfinished business—especially from a parent-child relationship. We think: "We are now adults." Ha!

While it is important to have one's own inner house in order (or be consciously trying to clean it up) before marrying and/or child-rearing, in actuality our closets are inhabited by "phantoms" who refuse to depart and continue to influence us. We cannot escape, through avoidance or ignorance, the effects of our roots, our past, our formative, primary, earliest relationships. Patterns formed early seem almost like stamps upon the soul. While I know this, I forget or it gets buried until something occurs to help me see and learn it anew. Cleaning house is an endless task.

We all carry a model, often it is a parent or a parental figure, against whom we compare and contrast our marriage partners. It is natural and inevitable. It is a major part of our unfinished business. Our dialogue about support is tied into male/female role models, as well as childhood influences. Charles Thomas's mother's priorities were few and clear: her husband and her children. Their needs took precedence over her own—or, put another way, there was less distinction between whose needs were whose. Her primary need was to help her family, to meet their needs. Supporting her husband meant putting him first.

Charles Thomas, like many of us, may say he realizes he does not want a spouse who will follow in the footsteps of his role model—his mother. Yet on a deeper level, we can't help but be governed to a degree by this early imprinting. Since we instinctively shrink away from change, our first response is often to reject as inadequate a model different from a parental one. Thus, Charles Thomas sometimes feels that I am not supportive enough. It may be because, among other reasons, I am different from his mother. Again, conscious recognition of this influence is a vital first step because these influences often remain unconscious. Then we need to reprogram ourselves with an updated message.

With my husband, as with my mother, I have not wanted to risk their disapproval or disappointment by expressing some of my needs. Their support and love was too important to risk. Instead of expressing needs they might not understand or agree with, I tried to fit into their schemes. What began with my mother continued with my mate, unconsciously. The unsettling part of this old pattern is that we are usually unaware of repeating it. It just happens. We think differently with new lovers, new children. In truth, we rarely are. Old patterns get reenacted.

Before I became a mother, I was very uncertain and worried about what sort of parent I would make. In my early twenties while I was actively trying to heal the painful relationship with my father, I carried a good dose of resentment, hostility, and anger toward him. As I recognized in myself some qualities I did not admire in my father, I was loath to pass any on to children we might bear.

Yet I had two—not one—parenting role models—two very different models. My mother was supportive, nurturing, patient, understanding, ready to listen, a peacemaker. My father was opinionated, volatile, impatient, ready to talk and expound, an inciter. Two very different personalities and role models. While I was attracted to my mother's example, I felt my instinctual responses more closely mirrored my father.

After six years in a relationship with Charles Thomas, I hadn't resolved this ambivalence, but I felt ready to jump in and try the waters of parenthood. Acknowledging these unresolved areas felt like an acceptable beginning. Four years and two children later, I was suffering from self-condemnation. Was this a self-fulfilling prophecy? My quiet anguish was due to a pervasive sense of inadequacy as a mother. Every other mother I knew appeared confident. I may have appeared so, too, but *rarely* did I feel it.

The Cayce readings expressed my ideals as a parent, but not my realities. Nonetheless, I discovered some guideposts in the "fine print" of readings for parents, perhaps because I wanted and needed to see and find such reassurance. On the one hand, the readings spoke frequently of "manifesting the fruits of the spirit" and of "being channels of blessings," which was discouraging to one so often as impatient as I. Yet they also repeated over and over that the greatest example and teacher and role model is one who is *true to oneself.* Other times, the advice was cloaked in terms of self-acceptance or doing one's best, or living true to one's own ideals and standards.

When I decided to take that to heart—to believe in myself and live it—I dare say that was a major turning point for me as a parent. It is a continuing process to sort through, when appropriate, in context, what is carried over from childhood, to honor the positive and let go of the negative. Cleaning house *is* endless! Yet I grow less ashamed of who and how I am. My children and I agree that I am prone to be impatient or that I get angry more than their dad. I think we are all relieved to speak about it openly. We agree we don't like it, that it's something I try to "do better," that they still love me! (Likewise, I hope they are experiencing that they are loved through thick and thin.)

While I often observe others who seem disappointed when the Cayce readings so often repeat phrases such as, "The answer must be found within self" or "Look within," my reaction is the opposite. I find tremendous reassurance and reinforcement in the admonition to trust myself, to depend on my own instincts. The desire to improve goes hand in hand with acceptance of who, how, and where I was and where I am now.

The value we place on friends and family, employees and

colleagues in our molecule, makes them worthy of some care and attention. Otherwise, as most easily evidenced with one's children, their influence can slip up unawares, so that only when there is a problem or crises is any attention given.

When our younger child was a little over a year old and the older girl was two, their father and I hit a low point—or, put another way, we had let the demands of work and children dominate us—seeping energy away from each other imperceptibly until we realized one day we felt too much like work partners. Beyond dealing with the children and talking about them, we had little to say to one another and not enough energy left to do much about it.

We "took stock" and admitted the problem: that much of the life and the spark of our relationship was dwindling to an all-time low. It was scary to admit it, but worse to think it and not share it! Somehow once it was out on the table, it became more manageable. It was easier to take action.

Now, seven years later, we continue to feel that the action taken back then was a real saving grace for our relationship. We reminded each other of our ideals, set years before, in which we agreed that the life and love in our family begins with the life and love between us; that our relationship needed to be fed so that we could most successfully nurture the children. We set aside time in our weekly schedule in the form of one evening and Saturday mornings out alone together.

When we have a minimum of a few hours alone together, we can connect in ways that are simply impossible when we are apart or when telephones, children, and chores interrupt at any moment. There is a tangible difference when interruptions are excluded. We share details of the week that went overlooked. We can move beyond the business of living together to more reflective sharing—plans for the future, deeper thoughts on how we feel in the present, or going back to a past time still unresolved.

Invariably, when we return home we are closer, more grounded. We have touched base—our bases—and are refueled in a vital way.

As all forms of unfinished business are recognized and brought into conscious awareness, we are on a road toward freedom—more energy, more space, within ourselves and our relationships—to create anew. A new relationship does not begin with a marriage or with a statement of love and commitment. On a deeper level, it begins fresh each time we can toss out baggage that is archaic, that doesn't fit, and each time we embrace, accept another aspect of who/how we are in the present.

Those who are in our molecule do affect us and our primary relationship. We can either deal with these influences facing forward, with some awareness and preparation, or we can back into them, bump into them, crash into them!

Unfinished business with family is a gold mine should we choose to see it as such. Beneath the earth are gems of our personal healing. They lie seemingly dormant. They may, in fact, be twinkling, signaling for attention. We choose to acknowledge—how much?—when and why?

The fact is unfinished business affects us—with or without our acknowledgment. To face that is the first step to freedom. It frees our present relationship from being burdened with past issues and patterns. It frees us to begin to see who we really are once the baggage has been lifted.

6

༄

Stumbling Blocks
to Stepping-Stones

*T*urn stumbling blocks into stepping-stones. This well-worn, much-loved phrase was a response Edgar Cayce gave countless times concerning all sorts of problems. It means, in part, that the ideal is to focus on and emphasize the positive side of any difficult situation or person. It further indicates a transformative element: We are encouraged to analyze a difficult situation (i.e., the stumbling stone) for the opportunities for growth (stepping-stones) inherent within it. The readings clearly state that these opportunities *are always* there. To identify them is the task. When we can turn what was a stumbling block into a stepping-stone toward further growth, we have transformed it and are free of it. It loses its hold on us. In the process some important lessons are experienced about the power of the mind, specifically the will, and of the spirit.

The truth of this was brought home to me by an experience with my husband a year or two after we were married. We were planning a weekend business trip to Florida. For a while prior to the trip my attitude toward Charles Thomas had been increasingly critical, revolving around a basic view that he was insensitive to me. I kept seeing ways in which this was true! New and more ways! Although I didn't voice half of what I was thinking, many of my comments were negative and my black mood was evident. The morning of our departure, Charles Thomas said, "I think you'd be happier staying home. I can't seem to do anything to please you."

I was startled. Taking stock of my attitude, I suddenly *knew* that my faultfinding could be never-ending. Quite decisively, I chose to relinquish it. I told Charles Thomas I'd be joining him and bringing along a different attitude.

The next evening in Florida, business completed, we were walking together quietly. In appreciating our quiet time together, I found myself appreciating Charles Thomas's quiet and gentle ways—and appreciating being out from under the black cloud of criticizing.

(While that example makes it sound so pat and easy to turn a destructive attitude into a positive one, it is a dramatic example of what is possible. This "simple" truth is usually more difficult, complex, and a never-ending challenge.) There are *always* new stumbling blocks that put us to the test—if we are alert or detached enough to see them as opportunities.

There were in addition many Cayce readings that counseled individuals to work on themselves first and foremost, and not try to change a troublesome loved one or friend.

When a reading simply said, "Analyze self" or "You are meeting self," it nonetheless left many people to figure out what that really meant for them. I don't think that "Analyze self" means "Justify self," as in coming up with all the seemingly sound, logical reasons that support one's own viewpoint.

Closely analyzing self means asking: Why is this (person, situation, attitude, etc.) a stumbling block to me? In other words, what does this situation teach me about me? That is what is meant by "meeting self." It is a radically different interpretation from the more typical one that holds others responsible for difficulties encountered.

As an adolescent, when tensions began escalating between my father and me, I was amazed, then later intrigued that my younger brother did not share my anger, resentment, hostility, and frustration. He reacted to our father quite differently, with less volatility and more restraint. I could not avoid the bald-faced truth hitting me over and over again: It was not my dad! He was not the intrinsic cause of all the trouble (to put it back into adolescent terms)! What I was really forced to face was that I had created this stumbling block by my response to him. Stumbling blocks do not only exist externally. They are just as often internal. Thus, relations with my father—or anyone—became my responsibility.

Stumbling blocks are actually highly individual, hand (mind)-crafted to suit our unique personalities. Looking at them, then, as stepping-stones means, often with great use of will, that they are viewed as keys to areas where we are stuck, where we could grow, where we could learn from letting go of a viewpoint that feels (but isn't) precious. Often what we believe most vehemently will get tied to a stumbling block. In other words, when we place too much importance on a goal—like making money, pursuing a career, achieving beauty, having a certain relationship—complications and conflicts often emerge. They may recur, like nagging nightmares, until positive learning transpires. This is one of the meanings of "God works in strange ways."

Charles Thomas and I heard M. Scott Peck, author of *The Road Less Traveled,* say in a marriage workshop, "There are two reasons to marry: One is to have children, the other is for friction." Friction is another word for stumbling blocks. Why would we want stumbling blocks? Stumbling blocks show us where we need to or could stand to grow, if we so choose. People are instead often stuck, stuck in patterns of relating or in negative attitudes because they (cannot) will not let go. Stepping-stones are born of letting go.

Sometimes it is the act of defining something as a stumbling block that is a major step toward turning it around, as with my experience before our Florida trip. The labeling itself frees us, gives the needed distance to see that there are options (stepping-stones), where earlier we were too enmeshed.

However, this process usually involves hard work and then letting go. It is hard work to attempt to alter one's perceptions of and responses to a difficulty. "Stumbling block" may be a gentle description of what appears to be a boulder. When all of our being wants to hate, hurt, reject, run away from an obstacle, it is *hard work*—an act of will—to choose instead the goal of transformation.

The letting-go aspect of the process seems to be essential for healing to occur. Implicit is an acknowledgment that with all healing—for that is a way of looking at this—we are not alone. We do our dead-level best and then are open to receive; we let go to "be" healed, helped, freed, and for the spirit to move.

A delightful teacher at A.R.E. for many years gave countless students the tool of saying, "Thank You, Father," all the time—no distinction was made between, and no greater value given to, good or bad events—it was all to be received with an ever-present "thank you." For me this is often a shortcut on the route to identifying stumbling blocks because, when it seems absurd or hard to say it, that is a clear indication that I've hit on one. The next step is to ask the question: "Why is this a stumbling block? What does it tell me about myself? What am I holding onto?"

Knowing an answer to these sorts of questions does not necessarily even facilitate a transformation, mind you. We've all had an experience of knowing what we "should" do or say (from an inner feeling, that is) when we also know we can't—not yet at least. Asking and answering such questions, however, does facilitate a healthy and honest self-analysis, essential to the process.

Crises and critical periods are the big stumbling blocks, the major obstacles, and stresses that put almost everyone to the test. This concept (turning stumbling blocks to stepping-stones) is about the big ones, and it is about the little ones. Its simple beauty is in its utility. It can be applied anywhere. The concept necessitates our taking a close, hard look at ourselves, unembarrassed to admit in the privacy of our solitude what are the big and little stumbling blocks, and then to start peering around for the clues to transform them into stepping-stones. For the clues are indeed there. There is always a way to look at a person/situation/oneself in a more speculative, different light. There is always something to learn about oneself. The catch is—do we really want to? Does it hurt enough to matter? Or do we care enough? Because these sorts of changes aren't easy and are often a matter of will—taking oneself by the scruff of the neck to shift a focus to a more positive, caring, open stance, when in fact we'd much rather justify all the valid reasons for our angers. It's much easier to excuse ourselves with comments like, "Oh, well. That's just the way I am."

Charles Thomas travels quite a bit. During the spring and fall seasons, it is common for him to be away one-half of all weekends. Naturally, this makes his days in the office busier, as work piles up in his absence. Time at the office is long and, when he's home, he's often tired and drained.

I remember very early in our relationship when he left on one of these trips—it was perhaps the first time I was left alone since we'd been together—I watched his car drive out of the driveway, then turned to an empty house and sank into the couch. The silence of the house was a stark reflection of the void I felt inside. It seemed the life and energy was driving away in that car. Long, solitary days loomed ahead, feeling endless. I probably wept, though I don't remember; it would fit! I probably also allowed some fears to creep in about being alone. I didn't know what to do with myself!

As I've stated, I had always thoroughly enjoyed time spent alone. Charles Thomas's departure that day did not mark my first experience with solitude. Consequently even in the midst of feeling that void, an inner voice was chastising me, with bemused detachment: "Oh, come on! Have you become so dependent?" I knew very early that travel would be a part of Charles Thomas's lifestyle. I could choose my response to that fact.

When that initial acute attack of loneliness subsided, two lessons (the stepping-stones) emerged. I believe they emerged sooner rather than later because I chose to stay in the solitude rather than fill the time alone with potentially distracting activity. By remaining alone, I chose a step toward analyzing my reactions and looking for lessons, one of which was: It was more than an indication of dependency. The intensity of the loneliness showed me how deeply I'd opened up to Charles Thomas. Secondly, the additional time alone and apart opened up great inner resources. Now, although children impinge upon that time, I continue to give a high priority to occasions when Charles Thomas is away. My best thinking, writing, praying, and openness to nature occur in solitude. I no longer experience these times of separation as negative in any way. My single-parenting falls into its own patterns and rhythms. The fatigue of it can often be eased with the help of friends. When they ask how we handle this "added stress," however, even the phrase does not fit my experience. Time spent at home when Charles Thomas is away is very different from when he's here—not better, not worse—simply different. I appreciate the contrast. What others interpreted as "added stress" has become, in my experience, a rejuvenating contrast. Like the example of my brother's differing response to my father, situations themselves are necessarily not inherently difficult nor stressful. Stumbling blocks can dissolve as our perceptions shift. I could blame Charles Thomas for leaving me too often (stuck in the stumbling block) or I can make myself look for the lessons, like arrows pointing toward growth.

Viewing difficulties in a marriage or a committed relationship, from the most trivial irritation to major differences, as potential stepping-stones is a major, major tool. The practice of placing blame and guilt is almost automatically (thankfully) laid to rest. The focus is properly centered upon each individual's inner perusal of attitudes.

Stepping-Stones Toward What?

Before I studied the Cayce readings my "worldview" was essentially humanistic, in line with Maslow's stages of growth toward a state of "self-actualization." [Abraham Maslow, the late psychologist and author, held the theory that there were basic or deficiency needs everyone needed to fulfill (such as human affection, security, self-esteem) before moving on to a concern with metaneeds, such as justice, goodness, beauty, and order. Individuals who had fulfilled metaneeds he called "self-actualized."] With this view alone, stepping-stones would be leading toward self or personal growth as the eventual goal or outcome. For me there was always something missing with that worldview. Self-actualization alone had a hollow ring to it.

The perspective in the readings added two dimensions that brought vitality, depth, and a feeling of "Aha! There's where I want to be headed!" These two dimensions are service and spirituality: a oneness with God. Personally, I am only partially attracted to self-growth as an end unto itself. Nor do I resonate to a totally outer-directed goal of serving. Combine the two as a path toward a state of consciousness that integrates a spiritual dimension and my spine tingles—life experiences become charged with meaning! So stepping-stones are like "enhancers of personal growth" toward soul development and fulfilling one's life purpose!

We have all had moments when we felt we "see with new eyes." Seeing the concept of turning stumbling blocks into stepping-stones as a way of growing toward soul development was such an experience for me. When the Cayce readings so often refer to Deuteronomy 30 because of the challenge, "I have set before you life and death, blessing and curse; therefore choose life," (v. 19) I hear that as an admonition to choose to (1) transform the stumbling blocks and (2) grow on a spiritual path.

This concept or tool is so powerful because of this implicit interplay between hard work and transformation, akin to a divine presence or a healing element. Let us not underestimate what happens when a transformation occurs: To be liberated where we were once in (emotional) chains is an essence of healing and transformation. It means that a wealth of energy—once stuck—has been freed up. This energy can then be turned toward more positive constructive uses. With that final choice, growth—choosing life—occurs. We grow in wisdom, humility, patience—nothing less than the fruits of the spirit.

7

Fruits of the Spirit

*B*eing reared in a nonpracticing Jewish home, I was un-
familiar with the phrase "fruits of the spirit" until as a
young adult I read the Cayce readings and, later, the New
Testament. I was immediately inspired by their call to practice the fruits of the spirit in individual lives—"just be kind,
be gentle; here a little, there a little."

I have interpreted the phrase to mean the naturally oc-
curring byproducts of psychological spiritual growth. Fruits
of the spirit, then, are such qualities as kindness, gentleness,
compassion, patience, long-suffering, hope, peace, love. The
list is as endless as these wonderful attributes.

Judging others by what they *do,* not by what they say is also seeing the fruits of the spirit. Actions speak louder than words. Is an individual giving to others? If so, it is a fruit of the spirit—God in action—a natural outpouring of a desire to be of service.

Since becoming a parent, I have been repeatedly struck by how beautifully infectious and contagious these attributes are as reflected in children. I can walk through two essentially identical situations with one of our girls, such as getting dressed, but with different attitudes. One day I will respond with patience and kindness and the event goes smoothly; the next time around I am frustrated and impatient and a struggle ensues! The results are almost predictable. As the girls grow older, the process can also work in reverse: In their kindness, they bring out kindness in me— more of an adult-to-adult situation. Such is the simple beauty of how the fruits of the spirit work in our relationships. The challenge is greatest, of course, when we don't *feel* kind or gentle or patient, etc., but are tired and cross.

There are subtleties and paradoxes inherent here. For example, it assuredly does not work to feign kindness or patience. That usually backfires.

If I am upset and sharing my feelings with Charles Thomas, he is often unnerved by my show of emotion. As a way of distancing himself, he has sometimes taken on a seemingly kind approach. It goes like this: "Oh, do you need to talk? Oh, sure. Get it all off your chest. I'll listen." "OK. Do you have anything else you need to say? Are you sure you're finished?"

Charles Thomas is far more kind to me when he is authentic and expressing his true feelings than when he is withholding or censoring the uncomfortable, painful truth. When viewed this way, trying to demonstrate fruits of the spirit does not mean repressing, ignoring, or overlooking negativity nor the complexities of emotions. Instead, it has come to mean to me: searching for the most loving, truthful response at any given moment. Long-suffering: " . . . though you be persecuted, unkindly spoken of, taken advantage of by others, you do not attempt to fight back or to do spiteful things; that you be patient—first with self—then with others . . . " (3121-1)

"Love is the giving out of that within self." (262-44) Faith, hope, patience, long-suffering, brotherly love, kindness, gentleness—these are the fruits of the spirit.

When I feign patience with our children, it is immediately expressed as sarcasm. The most obvious example is the old "I'm waiting" singsong, through gritted teeth. There are endless variations on that theme, but it's not a theme on patience.

Children are notorious for relentlessly testing parental limits. As parents, we are regularly getting our patience tested, but so, too, our powers of *discernment.* When is it the most loving response to be clear and firm about the limits and boundaries? After we "lose it" by being too firm, too angry, or too impatient, what is the most loving action to take to recover?

It is with these daily challenges and choices before us here—in the trenches, in the daily interactions—that an application of fruits of the spirit belongs.

On a good day, there are some quiet solitary moments upon waking. On a good day, I remember to use this time to pray a bit, to say an affirmation of an ideal: that I be "used as a channel of blessing this day." Or more specifically that I "respond to each opportunity with the highest in me." Or "give my children the care they each, individually, need." Or "be gentle, kind, helpful." By starting the day with these reminders ringing in my ears, I don't feel quite so alone and I have a sense of direction, rather than being tossed about in reaction to the day's events.

Sometimes, these are an integral part of my lifestyle.

Sometimes I remember to *pause* at various times throughout the day! When our six-year-old daughter refused to eat,
saying, "I don't have to. You're not the boss of me"; when I
remembered to *pause* before responding, progress began
on living with the fruits of the spirit. When I pause, something special happens, *even if* there is absolutely no apparent difference in the outcome of the situation. In the
moment of reflection, a tiny prayer goes out like a ripple
through the layers of mind and starts a different process. It
may be invisible to others, but I am an ounce clearer and
calmer in my responses. I am a tiny bit more aware of what
my daughter really needs or is requesting. I can hear the
music between the lines a bit more clearly.

Many times when I am embroiled in a dispute with one
of the children, I suddenly remember to pause, shaken by
how fast and furious the conversation has turned into a
struggle. Our child can be demanding, and reasoning does
not hold any water with her. She grasps all too well the reasons, yet is undaunted by them. It is at such times I need to
pause. I turn inward for help, feeling alone and fearful that I
am only going to mess this one up further. At these times, in
the moment's reflection, I simply ask to be guided, to be
used in the most helpful way. There are no hard and fast
rules nor pictures of what prayers and fruits of the spirit look
like. Sending a child to her room three times in a day may
be a kind response; it may even be executed in a gentle, yet
firm way.

The readings define long-suffering in a way I can understand and use: though you are persecuted or taken advantage of, you do not become spiteful or fight back.

Applied to child rearing, this advice comes alive, for children seem to take advantage frequently. As parents, we usually don't become spiteful because we realize that it is
unintentional or is their way of testing limits, experiment-
ing to see if manipulation works. Their awareness of others

is limited, still maturing. Parenting provides many opportunities to practice long-suffering, and this can be used as a
yardstick when applied to adult relationships. I choose to
see children in an ultimately positive, growth-seeking light,
not as devious or out-to-get-us adults. Much of the time
young ones (one to ten years of age) "push our buttons" as
an experiment—learning what actions evoke what responses. Realizing this helps us not to fight back or become
spiteful. Teaching them the consequences of their actions
requires us to be long-suffering and show patience, both
fruits of the spirit.

As a parent, I often wonder if (and wish that) another
"fruit of the spirit" might be called "humanness" or "self-
acceptance." During incidents when I am "less than perfect" and fail to respond with kindness, patience, or mercy,
but react instead of respond, I wonder what this demonstrates to the children. My comfort and consolation is to
share with the girls my continued attempts to "do better."
By admitting openly and honestly that I am fallible, often
wrong and mistaken, often sorry and regret my actions, I
am admitting my humanness, learning, and teaching self-
acceptance. Teaching our children to be self-accepting is
just as valuable as patience. I am practicing for myself and
modeling for them patience with oneself, kindness toward
oneself, unconditional love that says, "I admit when I've
fallen, I'm sorry. I'm working with myself. Let's all forgive
me." Each time I embrace them after a struggle, we all learn
more about forgiveness. Accepting ourselves each step
along the way while keeping an eye on our common goal is
a process the children and I are in together. I am trying to
bring fruits of the spirit down to earth, as handles to grasp
all along the way, even when we falter because we are human.

Another more subtle fruit of the spirit, to me, is humor.
So often when a power struggle is imminent and brewing

with one of the children and when I am tired and irritable, Charles Thomas can switch on a figurative light bulb by saying or doing something silly. Like spring rain our laughter washes us clean. Laughing at ourselves so often can free us from the snares of a negative pattern. I've had vivid occasions when Charles Thomas is traveling, I am tired after a day of single parenting, and we are all irritable. My bones seem to be calling to me to simply lighten up the situation—that's all—to just step out of the downward cycle of an ensuing argument with a tickle or a joke. While I often feel too tired to use it, I know that humor and levity are ever accessible, like gifts or treats ready to be opened. They so often transform a potentially heavy circumstance into fun.

One other element that *feels* like a fruit of the spirit, though isn't one of those usually mentioned, revolves around the beauty and sacred elements in nature and in the arts. Again, these are transformative elements. Like a sprinkling of kindness, a sunset can raise consciousness and wonderment in an instant!

Charles Thomas and I love to travel, yet it hasn't come easily and naturally for us to travel together. Our instincts and styles are at variance: I am the more tense and precise, he easygoing and loose. Many times we have found ourselves sorting out these differences while traveling, wishing we were just having a great time. But then as we enjoyed Impressionist paintings or a beautiful city or a delicious meal, we were almost always lifted out of the rut we'd fallen into. The experience moved us to another place; that is, the tensions between us were gently eased by the beauty of our experience. That may be more a "gift" than a fruit of the spirit. In any case, it is sad and unfortunate that it is all too easy to overlook or forget about these gifts or tools that are *always at hand!*

My miscarriage was not my first prolonged period of withdrawal. The early months of my first two pregnancies were two other occasions. After I went bumbling through the first pregnancy's initial trimester and alienated Charles Thomas, he was better prepared and less alarmed the second time. Needless to say, I was not very sensitive to him during those months when I felt so ill. However, in the months following the miscarriage and during times of withdrawal, I felt able and wanted to reach out, to maintain contact, albeit minimal, with Charles Thomas. Quite consciously, I chose physical proximity and affection as the vehicle. While I didn't have a lot to say, not much energy for initiating conversation or activity, touching and closeness felt right. The warmth of bodily contact instinctively felt healing in several ways: He didn't feel so abandoned or shut out, I didn't feel as cold or numb. I felt close somehow, accepted and accepting somehow—all on an unspoken level.

There are many books written now on the healing powers of touch. It seems to be another transformative element—a fruit of the spirit?—readily available and accessible, all too often forgotten along the way. After those empty months, when I relied so heavily on touch for renewal—and gradually felt it—I gained renewed respect for it and an added sense of wonder: What makes it so powerful, in its gentle, unassuming way? Like the inner workings of patience and gentleness and all fruits of the spirit, there is a real sense of mystery surrounding touch, humor, and "humanness." When they are in action, magic feels nearby.

Why is it that we are "in the flow" sometimes and not other times? Clearly it is a mystery, yet there is also much we can consciously choose to do to foster, nurture, and strengthen fruits of the spirit in our lives.

It needs to be said that the foundation upon which the fruits of the spirit rest has to do with putting others first. More than an awareness of, a sensitivity to others, this truly means turning the other cheek—putting others first. When I think back to moments when I felt truly patient as a mother, it has been when I was listening to our daughter—not muddied with my own inner voice. Not realizing or articulating it at the time, I was putting her first, perceiving her need at the moment, not making her fit into my needs.

How do we invoke the fruits of the spirit into the daily workings of our lives? Just as my journey to make changes in patterns with my father took a combination of work and prayer, these are the two elements I call upon here. It is also the process referred to in chapter 3 with slightly different words: Work on self, let it go (akin to prayer).

Being by nature somewhat assertive and outspoken and somewhat intense and goal oriented, I have found that gentleness and patience do not come as easily and naturally to me as to Charles Thomas. Over the years I've soul-searched and self-condemned over this. I've devoted periods of earnest effort that were focused on trying to be more gentle and patient. The results seem to be a smattering of ups and downs. It is an ongoing challenge—like choosing to stay on a healthy diet. But my brothers and parents, who "knew me when" and see me only intermittently now, often comment on the changes they see. Their unsolicited remarks are encouraging, especially when I feel as though I am spinning my wheels. It seems clear that whatever our natural tendencies, we can access the fruits of the spirit by earnest effort. I realized this recently when our older child was going through a period of increased anxiety about being left at home without either parent—even for an evening. My intuition told me she was not being manipulative. During one week when her distress was most acute, she began crying in the late afternoon about the prospect of going to bed without me nearby. Every day, moaning and wailing. While I did not change her bedtime routine, most of the time I felt compassion and sympathy instead of impatience. I tried to comfort her. Toward the end of that week I recognized how atypical my response was. I had

been patient without "trying to be patient." It was so refresh-
ing to just see it be my response without forethought. Recognizing my natural tendency toward impatience, I feel
sure that my patient response was the cumulative effect of
prior work.

In order to allow the spirit to cleanse me of past habits
and move me to a new space in my life, and the effects of
prayer to be felt, I need time alone. This goes beyond the
benefits of momentarily pausing in the midst of turmoil.
Reserving regular uninterrupted blocks of time alone gives
the silence necessary for prayer. If Charles Thomas and I
are distant or disputing, it is critical for us to make quiet
time, during which feelings and questions can be seen more
clearly. During this period, more important feelings beneath the surface reveal themselves and the problem often
falls away or back into proper proportion, sometimes taking the outer event or issue with it, for it was often petty.
Taking such time is being kind and gentle to oneself, to one's
important relationships, to those dear to us.

It is not easy to act with kindness or gentleness where
we've been or are hurt, to swallow our pride and admit our
mistakes or regrets. But for love, with love, in love—we must.
Like most risks, it looks and feels so much harder and more
scary before we take it. Deciding to assume the risk of
changing a habitual response with one of these fruits of the
spirit is the hardest step of the process. Once taken, we begin to reap the exquisite rewards of truly being how we were
meant to be—channels of blessings here, now, to those that
we contact day by day.

8

⚬

Service to Others

*T*he birth of our first child, as most parents can appreciate, was a huge leap into the world of service! Parenthood is such a lovely way to be introduced to the true meaning of putting another's needs before your own. It is a gradual and gentle exposure to adulthood in a new light. There is almost an unspoken affinity especially among new parents, but among all parents—a knowing look in the eye that gleams the coded message: Yes, we both know. I, too, have been there. What we now know is our firsthand and thorough initiation into a deeper, pure experience of service.

Until I became a parent, much as I valued being thoughtful and considerate of others' needs, when all else was stripped away, I did come first. It is understandable, natural in a way. An infant's presence, supplemented, no doubt, by biological, hormonal changes, alters that consciousness forever. It is no small miracle. Tasting, swallowing, and digesting what it's like to truly put another's needs before mine—and that includes the joys as well as the sacrifices—has been one of the most powerful lessons in my life so far.

Now that our children are older, this experience of practicing service feels less intense, but the deeper understanding it brought remains. The real challenge is to apply the ever-present opportunity to "put another first" to our marital relationship, to our extended family, to our colleagues, and finally to each situation in which we find ourselves.

Individual Expressions of Service

The real clincher for me has to do with attitude. The Sufi Order, in so many of its powerful dances, uses chants that are variations on a theme of "the God in me greets the God in you." When I feel this, all the superficial feelings of obligation ("I should do good; I should help those less fortunate") fall away. The Cayce readings, too, have emphasized this shift in focus, with their consistent nudge to give a little here, a little there, where you are today. When I am mentally quiet enough to see with new eyes the minute everyday evidence of the Spirit of love, the urge to serve—to add a positive spark to any situation—spontaneously comes forth. That is the ideal—to see, feel, act with that clarity and love, to add a positive spark.

Like maintaining a healthy diet, this response means day-to-day choices. If you've gotten this far in this book, it has probably already been evident—as now—how circular and interconnected these concepts and ideas are. Ideals are a vehicle for prioritizing and focusing on whatever is most important, such as service and forgiveness. Turning stumbling blocks into stepping-stones is another vehicle for adjusting perception, turning our lens, our viewpoint, to see any situation as a potential lesson, a chance to make choices, to respond according to our ideals.

Taking quiet time regularly to pray and/or meditate is another tool to move toward living our ideals. For in the silence I can feel more clearly my individual path toward service, which for me is critical. Service is something we are indoctrinated about so that to move past the indoctrination toward my personal relationship with service, I have needed quiet. First, there was the statement of the ideal: Yes, we want service to be an integral part of our relationship and lives. Now, second, for me: What is my/our "right relationship" to service?

I have a close friend who is very committed to social action, particularly to service focused on the underprivileged, and who holds Mother Teresa as her model. My husband, equally committed to spiritually based service of a different sort, like my friend, strives daily to meet personal standards of selfless giving. These are two people in my life who embody "right relationship" with service. Right relationship, by definition, means right for them. It has been uniquely defined, not according to predetermined requirements.

The Cayce readings define service as *giving*. Period. That is simple, precise, and yet affords the leeway for individual interpretation.

I'm now in this second stage of uncovering my right relationship with service, specifically within our marriage. How I defined service five or ten years ago doesn't seem to fit now. This is not a fixed but a fluid relationship. I suspect it is to be continuous—learning what it means to give, to be willing to go more than halfway. I—we—seek to discover, uncover the ways of giving that correspond with who I am. All along the path there are temptations to accept, to wear a religious and/or cultural interpretation of service. These temptations are both real and subtle.

Reared within the Jewish tradition, I am familiar with the concept of "right action." That tradition places high value on doing good works. Yet, even as a child, I stumbled over the realities of doing what "appeared" to be good as opposed to giving out of a sincere, caring attitude. As an adult, I am still sorting this out, still have a personal bias toward achieving right attitude as a precursor to right action.

Which brings me back to the inadvertently perfect lessons on service built into the world of parenthood. Being a mother was my first true experience of service based solely on love—at last, my attitude was right—and of spontaneous giving with no thought of receiving or recognition. Motherhood inspires a pure desire to give, unfettered by any prior conditioning, and an experience of such giving being its own reward.

The challenge of the Cayce readings and the Bible is to set as an ideal *whatever is our personal notion* of service as clearly as possible. We, at least, then know our goal. Then, we take incremental steps toward that ideal, especially in our closest relationships. A tall order!

Personal Struggles with Service

My struggles with service or giving have meant making myself get outside of the natural inclination to focus first on my needs, desires, and wants. Instead, I have (with and without moderate success) turned attention to Charles Thomas (or a close friend or other family member). More specifically, I have turned quiet reflective attention there—to watch for, listen, and finally respond to their needs.

I don't mean to simplify a complex, deep dynamic. We are never all self-centered nor all other-focused. We are now in that gray area of nuances and subtleties, difficult to discern, much less grasp. In this gray area and with a much-needed dose of self-detachment and observation, often I see my first instinct to be self-centered most of the time. Again, quiet times (meditation and prayer) facilitate and stimulate a much-needed slowing-down process, so one's first instinct needn't be the one acted upon.

To take a hypothetical example, if Charles Thomas calls at 5:00 p.m. saying that he's bringing home supper guests, my mental process goes roughly like this:

> *First Phase:* I have had a hard day, too. I can't pull this together in time. He is inconsiderate. I am too tired to entertain.
> *Second Phase:* Stop. Listen. Remember.
> *Third Phase:* He must have a good reason. So what if dinner is lacking and the house is not the cleanest. Even though I'm tired, I don't need to say or do a lot, just listen. It's not that big a deal.

The third phase is full of important factors. The idea that "he must have a good reason" is a variation on a theme in the readings: Everything is purposeful. Therefore, "if Charles Thomas doesn't have a good reason, then the Creative Forces do!" It's the familiar "stepping-stone in every stumbling block" idea. The final sentence is also critical. I've felt myself move more readily toward a giving attitude when I have asked myself: How important is this? Usually, if I remember to think that "it's not that big a deal," then it's not too hard to be of service rather than resist the opportunity.

A more complex opportunity for me was provided by our younger daughter, who for many years had difficulty going to sleep or staying asleep at night. This was particularly hard on me because not only was I fatigued, I also relished uninterrupted time alone. I cherished nighttime space and freedom. So, I had little patience for and much resistance to her requests, demands, reasons. I felt as though she were cross-ing over a boundary, invading my personal domain.

One of my stock phrases was, "No, you cannot have an-other kiss. Enough is enough." Well, all during these times, our older daughter, the one seeking peace and harmony, would quietly encourage me to give her younger sister what she wanted. But it took me quite a while to question my way of handling it. I discovered that our sage child was in-deed right. By giving the younger child what she requested, the episodes were short-circuited and soon petered out. The power play ended when I stopped struggling and of-fered no resistance. There was no resistance. I gave in—a telling pun. In learning to give (in) more, I dare say I may be learning something in general about giving and service. Certainly a very similar lesson came with the experience with my father. Patterns of conflict were released when I "gave in" and received what the situation was presenting rather than resisting it.

So the question, "Is this a big deal?" is pivotal, for when the answer is, "Yes, this is really important," one needs to be sure that the response is not a selfish one and a step away from service.

To give, with no thought of return, is devalued, over-looked perhaps because it is scary. We are vulnerable and we open ourselves to be taken advantage of, be it by a child, spouse, client, stranger. Culturally, giving has been coupled with weakness. "You didn't stand up for yourself; you gave in," we are told. Or "You can't give unconditionally, to just anyone, or you'll be taken advantage of." We are counseled to keep tabs, "Hey, I 'gave' at the office," or in a marriage, "We did what you wanted the last three times. Now it's my turn." The message ingrained has been: If you don't look out for yourself, no one else will. This guarded, self-protective, defensive stance looks upon the notion and challenge of giving with deep wariness and skepticism.

Yet, it is basically simple: To the extent that we can, we are called to give. When there is a knock at our door, we are called to answer. It seems there is something vital in responding with giving.

Again, reflecting a moment more on a cultural level, it seems that the fascination and inspiration evoked in so many by Mother Teresa goes far beyond the socialized norm of "service is good." Many experience through her example an intimate taste of a sacred element in selfless giving or, put another way, unconditional love. It challenges us to examine more honestly our relationship with service, with giving.

In committed relationships we are inevitably and repeatedly called to give. What's more, it is usually in just the ways and areas that are the most difficult, which is why family life is often termed a more strenuous path of spiritual development. With or without the dimension of parenthood, we are best "shown"—through situations with loved ones—where we are stuck, holding on, and—as such—where we need to let go, to give, to serve. So when I examine why I get so angry with Charles Thomas or with one of the girls, it is frequently because I don't want to give—in some way or another.

Changing both the cultural messages and childhood confusions regarding what service means and its place in daily life is most assuredly a slow and tedious process. My habits and instincts are first self-centered. As a parent, I may speak of caring for and consideration of others, yet frankly it is no doubt a mixed message of the sort that I, too, received as a child. Nevertheless, the readings' reassurances to "start where you are," "here a little, there a little" have helped to keep me focused on the importance of the little things, the daily efforts more in the direction of giving.

Meditation and Service

Perhaps one of the hardest, most challenging aspects of bringing service into personal, daily living is to wake up to the knocks on the door. To see and hear the opportunities to give is crucial, deceptively simple yet amazingly hard. I find I am dense, set in my ways of seeing and perceiving. Take the example of my daughters at bedtime. It took a long time and was quite a major change for me to even perceive that situation as an opportunity to "learn service" or to give. I've no idea of all the comparable situations that were unheard "knocks" on the door of my consciousness. It is a vital benefit of regular meditation and/or quiet time that it provides the space for sensitizing oneself, so that such knocks are to be heard. Setting service as an ideal is an acknowledgment that we want to hear and respond to service opportunities knocking on our door. Deciding to take time regularly, to be alone and quiet, is a natural next step for me, for I am crowded and noisy internally. It is not easy to see typical, daily relationships or situations in a new light. Even when a light may dawn, there's an inexorable pull back toward the previous old, familiar ways of reacting and perceiving. It can get discouraging. I so often feel just as self-centered as ever.

To embrace a more comprehensive view, a more optimistic one, is instead to see that: Yes, we may be self-centered at times. Yet, we are turned in the direction of giving and of loving. And each time we get turned around, with persistence we will yet again and again turn toward a life of giving, willing to risk, yes, and willing to trust that truly nothing is lost as we are learning to love and give—each in his or her own unique way.

Part III

Sensitive Issues in Love Relationships

— *Charles Thomas Cayce* —

9

Money Management

Money is often cited as the most common stumbling block in marriages and other relationships. There's every indication that financial issues are becoming a more prevalent cause of stress as our society moves toward the twenty-first century. There are a number of reasons for this trend, particularly in our current Western social system.

I think one major cause of modern financial stress is the pervasive message we receive from so many sources, particularly advertising and our perceptions of people around us, that material possessions will make us happy. We're continually exposed to scenes of couples and friends enjoying "the good life" in various luxurious living situations—vacation spots, restaurants, automobiles, and so on. These images combine to transmit the message that the more wealth and possessions we have, the happier we'll be.

I feel that this picture leads to a good deal of dissatisfaction in many lives, for it is basically an inaccurate one. Like many other sources, the Edgar Cayce readings state that material success does not guarantee happiness. Many people who sought guidance on their financial situations were given advice like the following: " . . . know that material things alone do not bring contentment—they only bring contention, unless harmony and peace abide also with [them]." (1965-1) The point here is not that money is evil. But if we believe that just having a certain amount of the world's goods will in itself make our lives continuously and intensely enjoyable, we are setting ourselves up for serious disappointment.

The unrealistic expectation that our lives can move without interruption from one peak experience to another reminds me of a feeling I sometimes get from visitors to our little farm. As we talk about raising animals and vegetables, it seems that some of these people see the end product and that is all they see. Little attention is paid to the day-to-day effort necessary to produce a bountiful garden and healthy, prolific farm animals. This is just one example of our society's tendency to focus on the "quick fix," the end result. When this attitude is brought to the financial aspect of a relationship, it can cause an unwillingness to pay attention to the less exciting processes involved in managing money on a daily basis.

There are several other ways in which gardening can serve as a useful analogy to economic considerations within a relationship. If two people are to work together productively on a garden, they have to communicate clearly with each other. Decisions must be made on how much time and energy they will devote to the garden and what crops they will grow in it. Similarly, the two partners in a relationship should reach clear agreements on how important money will be to them and what purposes it will serve in their lives.

In making decisions of this sort—whether in regard to a garden or the financial aspect of a relationship—each partner must be sensitive to the biases and patterns the other brings into the joint venture. Anyone who enters a relationship comes into it with certain attitudes and opinions about money already formed. These established mental patterns must be taken into account if a couple is to reach workable financial decisions.

Flexibility is another valuable quality. In gardening, one must be ready to make adjustments based on the weather, the choice of crops that will thrive in given soil conditions, and the amount of time and energy available for the project. A similar flexibility is needed in order to manage the financial side of a relationship successfully. At times it may be appropriate to change work situations, attitudes toward a job, or spending plans. We must be willing and able to make such adjustments when they are called for.

Gardening has also helped me learn to really appreciate the helpfulness of a balanced focus on the end result and the process leading up to that result. Most successful gardeners I know have grown to love the many steps leading to the end result of harvesting the produce. This, too, is something I feel can be applied to the material side of life. It's possible to build mental attitudes that will enable us to appreciate the process of making money as much as the end result of having it to use. Most of the people I've met who are really successful and happy in life have learned this secret of coming to enjoy the steps toward their goals, even as they are taking them.

So many of the messages prevalent in our society are focused on either reflecting on the past or planning for the future. The efforts and processes of the present somehow seem to get overlooked. For many of us, if we're not involved in some peak experience at the moment, the present becomes unimportant. We feel we need more, so we focus on our plans for the future and miss our chance to enjoy what's happening now.

Yet, to return to our example of the garden, we've found that being centered on the present does more than just create an awareness of the necessary operations of preparing the soil, sowing the seeds, and taking care of the developing plants; actual pleasure can be found in focusing on these steps. Somehow our current culture has produced a tendency to miss the pleasure and fulfillment that can be derived from each moment's activities. Our more active use of this old Eastern practice of valuing the process would help us rediscover our sense of joy in the present and thus eliminate much of our disappointment and frustration over money matters.

The feeling that being wealthier will make us happier is related to another characteristic of our modern lifestyles: the impulse to keep up with our neighbors. This can cause us to strive to acquire more and more material goods—including, in some cases, ones that we probably wouldn't feel we needed were it not for our tendency to compare what we have with the possessions of the people around us. The result, of course, is increased expenditures, which can add unnecessary financial stress to a relationship.

Several Edgar Cayce readings consider the question of how to avoid letting the values of others dictate our decisions regarding our use of money. The recommended first step is to formulate our ideals clearly. This will enable us to base our choices on our own perception of what is best, rather than allowing ourselves to be pulled in contradictory directions by outside influences. In the context of a relationship, if a couple can agree what is truly important to them, they will be more likely to use their material resources in ways that enhance the quality of their association.

Making financial decisions that are in line with our ideals may occasionally prove difficult, especially when these choices don't fit in with society's predominant standards. One Cayce reading that examined this dilemma in some detail states unequivocally that in such cases public opinion should be disregarded. The reading acknowledges that doing so can lower one's status in the eyes of others, for "in a material world material conditions are [the standard by] which individuals or others judge an individual's success..." (520-2) Nevertheless, our basic choice regarding money is described in clearly defined terms: "... there is today set before thee good and evil. Choose that which would be well-spoken of by others for the physical gains, or that which will bring content, peace that passeth understanding from within..." (520-2)

It should be pointed out that neither the discourse quoted above nor the Cayce material in general is against money. Material goods can be very useful in enabling us to lead productive, fulfilling lives, and thus they have an undeniable role in both individual growth and the development of a relationship. The readings do not ignore the significance of financial questions, and they don't recommend that material wealth be renounced. What they do emphasize is the importance of keeping the proper perspective of the role of money in our lives. Financial resources are best seen as a means to an end, not an end in themselves.

This point is made in several readings that address the purpose behind our life's work. These readings suggest choosing employment not for the sake of becoming rich, but so that we can move toward our ideal. Not only will this outlook help us keep a balanced attitude toward money, it will actually enable us to receive a greater abundance of the world's goods. Perhaps the clearest statement of this principle is given in Cayce's reply to a person with musical ability who asked how this talent could be used to bring an increase of material assets: "If it's for the purpose of material assets alone, you are already through!" (622-4) But, Cayce continued, if the ability is used to create in people a desire to know the truth, "then it may go a *long* way in adding to thy material gains; but these *must* be the *results, not* the purpose or the cause of thy use of thy voice!" (622-4)

This concept is directly related to economic healing, a subject which was explored in the many readings given for people seeking financial advice. These discourses encouraged people to adopt helpful attitudes toward money, and they also provided specific recommendations on how individuals could meet their material needs. I feel that this guidance could prove very useful in relieving the financial pressures affecting so many modern relationships.

One of the most important points made in these readings is that the fear of poverty is a serious hindrance to prosperity. As one person was told, "It is the *fear* of this or that, that prevents a channel from making for the greater supply." (254-85) Evidently, as we allow the fear of lack to fill our minds, we close ourselves off from the sources of abundance that life would make available to us. This preoccupation with poverty, sometimes called poverty consciousness, can affect both rich and poor. For some poor, it can produce a type of paralysis that prevents people from taking advantage of their opportunities. And in the rich, it can lead to hoarding and the inability to enjoy or use productively the wealth that is available.

I repeatedly saw this fear in operation during an earlier period of my life, when I played poker. It was interesting to observe how certain players would freeze when the stakes got high and their stack of chips got low. They'd become conservative and try to play by different rules. Good players don't do this; they play each hand the same way, even if their supply of chips is low. But when the less skillful ones became afraid of running out of money, they would fail to bet the hands they should. This type of poverty consciousness affects people in all areas of life and prevents them from making full use of the resources they do have.

Recognizing the source of one's fear of poverty can be an important first step in overcoming it. In some cases, a person may have picked up a poverty consciousness from his or her parents, particularly if they showed a great deal of anxiety over the family's means. The person might then carry this characteristic into later life, where it would influence the financial side of any relationship.

A second possibility, suggested by the Cayce material on reincarnation, is that an individual's attitudes toward money and experiences with it originated in previous lifetimes. There are a number of ways in which this might happen. For example, several readings indicated that people were experiencing financial hardship in the present because they had misused their wealth during earlier incarnations. It is also conceivable that someone who had taken a vow of poverty in a previous lifetime might have created a pattern of lack that continues to influence the experiences today. When patterns like these are brought into a relationship, the situation can call for a great deal of sensitivity, especially from the partner of the person carrying them.

To meet such patterns effectively, whatever their origin, many of the readings on economic healing recommended maintaining an attitude of confidence and faith as we take active measures to fulfill our financial needs. As one person who was seeking a job that would provide economic independence was told: " ... most of all, do not lose faith in self nor self's abilities, when trusting in the divine influences that are the birthright of every soul." (78-7)

From the perspective of the Cayce material, this trust can be based upon the promise that those seeking to live according to God's plan need have no fear of want. Whatever is necessary for our spiritual growth, we will receive. One person was offered the assurance, typical of those given in a good number of readings, that "the silver and the gold are the Lord's, and He withholdeth nothing that is good from those who serve Him." (2506-1) Another was told, " . . . if [people] are attempting to live a normal life, if wealth is necessary for their soul development it is a portion of their experience!" (498-1)

The specifics of living in harmony with the divine plan are, of course, different for different individuals. But for each of us, the economic aspect of such a life would involve using our material resources to manifest God's love for others. Several readings suggested tithing, donating ten percent of one's income to a worthy cause, as an effective way of letting God's bounty flow through our lives.

I feel that adopting the positive, confident attitude toward money recommended in the Cayce readings and living in a way that reflects this faith would help many individuals overcome their poverty consciousness and enable them to make the most of their financial opportunities. Within a relationship, it would help both partners to meet the worry and anxiety over money that add so much strain to so many of today's marriages.

Recent statistics suggest that in two-thirds of the homes in the United States in which there are two adults, both are working at least part time. One of the reasons for this is the increased financial pressures of modern life. Another important factor, however, is the healthy tendency of women today to be more independent and to consider a wider range of vocational options, including those outside the home.

Beneficial as this trend may be, it can also produce a need for greater understanding between partners. As two sources of income become part of the picture, it often happens that each contributing partner will have a number of strong opinions about how the money should be spent. In many homes today, the era when the husband would simply give the wife a monthly allowance is long past.

This is just one illustration of the growing complexity members of modern society are facing in relation to money, as in so many other areas of life. Leslie and I have been formulating our own responses to such issues, using some of the basic concepts explored in the Cayce readings. As we've worked with the financial aspect of our lives and its effect on our relationship, three areas have emerged as being particularly important: common ideals, values, and goals with regard to money and material things; control issues concerning the use of money; and communication.

Common Financial Ideals, Values, and Goals

The process of setting ideals described in the Cayce readings can help us recognize the direction we'd like our lives and our relationships to take. Just as an ideals chart can be formulated for other areas of an association, one can be developed to cover the financial aspect as well. Doing so is an important step in addressing issues involving money that arise in the relationship.

Here is an abbreviated example of our ideals chart regarding money:

MONEY / FINANCIAL IDEALS

Spiritual	Mental (Attitudes)	Physical (Actions, Behaviors)
Giving	Detachment	Know what is needed and what is wanted/desired
Generosities	Balance	Monitor spending: how much is on non-necessities?
		Save 20% of income
		Donate 10% of income

A chart like this can help each of us focus on two crucial questions regarding the role of money in our lives:

What is important in my life?
How do I reflect those priorities through my use of money?

One way of identifying what is important to you is to ask yourself what six or eight things you'd want to be sure to get to safety if your house were burning. This can help you clarify which material possessions mean the most to you, and it can also enable you to see how significant physical things in general are in your life.

Another interesting little exercise will help you focus on where you are now in your attitudes and behavior toward money, as compared with where you'd like to be. It has been said that someone can tell what you value or think is important by what you spend your money on—or, to put it another way, where you spend your money is where your heart is. After you've made an ideals chart covering the financial aspect of your life, look back over your cancelled checks or sales receipts for the past several months. Determine how your actual spending compares to the ideals, values, and priorities reflected in your chart.

Once you've identified your own ideals, it can be very helpful for you to work with your partner on formulating your joint priorities related to spending. The point is for the two of you to build toward common ideals and goals with regard to your use of money. This can enable you to avoid some of the difficulties that sometimes arise in a relationship between two people whose financial value systems are different. By coordinating your ideals with each other's and then making an effort to act in conformance with those ideals, you and your partner can take a meaningful step toward building and maintaining harmony in the economic aspect of your relationship. An example of how this can work is described in Cayce's answer to a woman who asked for advice on overcoming her husband's lack of generosity:

"Let [this lady] be just as generous to the husband as she expects the husband to be to her, and these will be more in accord and will bring greater harmony in the relationships throughout the experience. These [people] each have ideals. Make them coordinate with the material, the mental and the spiritual lives of each." (3051-4)

Control

A great deal has been written about control issues, some subtle and some not so subtle, that arise in a relationship. Many of these questions are addressed through money. Does the pattern of control of the money in our relationship reflect broader patterns of control between us? Are there imbalances? If so, can we make adjustments here and have a positive effect on the whole set of control issues in a relationship? I think so. It is important for two people to talk about the issue of control in general in their lives together, and then to talk specifically about how their conclusions can be reflected in the way money responsibilities are shared between them. One thing you and your partner should each consider here is how important it is to you to be in charge of or involved in the financial aspect of your relationship. An honest discussion of this question can help guide you in making mutually satisfactory decisions about your respective financial responsibilities.

The area of control of money is one in which our feelings are often picked up from our parents. For example, someone raised in a home where it was expected that the major breadwinner would make most of the financial decisions might well bring this attitude into his or her relationship. Leslie and I have a friend who seems to fit this pattern. This woman feels that since her husband earns most of the money, she needs his permission before she can spend any significant amount of it. I don't believe this outlook is something her husband imposed on her. She just brought it with her from her own upbringing and it's taken her twenty years of marriage to finally start getting free of it.

In examining our attitudes toward money, it's important for us to be aware of where they come from. Are they authentically our own, or are they unconscious assumptions we brought with us from watching our parents? Recognizing the source of our feelings about money can help us determine how large a part we want each of them to play in the financial agreements we work out with our partners.

One widely recommended system of managing money in a relationship involves making a fairly clear distinction about which expenses are to be paid by which person. It is suggested that a couple establish this distinction in advance through a shared decision and that it be maintained by having four bank accounts: a joint savings account, a joint checking account, and a separate checking account for each person. Early in our own relationship, Leslie and I found that this arrangement worked quite well.

In the system we use, all the income each month is initially put into the joint checking account. From there, a predetermined amount is transferred to the joint savings account; the two people decide together how and when this money is to be invested or spent. At the beginning of each month, allocations are made from the joint checking account to each individual checking account. The sizes of these shares are based on the expenses to be covered by each person, as decided upon originally. An amount is also included in each portion to meet miscellaneous and contingency expenses, as is a discretionary amount for each one.

It may take a few months to get this sorted out, and adjustments will probably have to be made. These should be based on a review of expenditures at the end of each month.

One key is agreeing ahead of time, at the beginning of each month, about the individual expense responsibilities of each person. This agreement can be based upon the couple's stated financial ideals, values, and goals. And many couples find that their ideals regarding money become clearer as they discuss and reach a decision on how their financial resources are to be used.

Over the years our comfort and understanding of each other's attitude and practice with money has resulted in simplifying the bank accounts to two joint accounts

Communication

As with most other aspects of a relationship, effective communication regarding finances is important to the success of the association. But in some ways communication about money matters can be more difficult than about other areas of life. One reason for this is that financial issues may serve as a front or a substitute for other unresolved problems in the relationship.

One partner may use the subject of money to blame the other and try to make him or her feel guilty. Such behavior can be an expression of anger over something that actually has nothing to do with finances. Similarly, one person might use this area of a relationship to focus on and exaggerate something that he or she believes is a particular weakness of the other. For instance, a husband may feel that his wife generally doesn't pay enough attention to details or that she is too spontaneous in areas that don't necessarily involve money; but to drive his point home, he may criticize her for making purchases too quickly or for not consulting him in financial decisions.

Inappropriate blame can do a lot to block communication regarding money. This effect might be seen if the partner who takes the major responsibility for keeping detailed records and balancing the checkbook somehow regularly gets blamed for shortfalls. In such a case, this person could feel a natural inclination to avoid discussing the situation. Or maybe during periods of financial difficulty it's the one producing most of the income who gets criticized for not bringing in enough. For example, if in a marriage there is insufficient money to pay all the bills, a husband who is expected to be the main breadwinner may have a tendency to resist talking about the problem.

Avoiding this type of block regarding money depends upon effective communication in other areas. It's most healthy for problems and difficulties to be discussed in relation to their actual causes. The key is to not let the financial aspect of a relationship become the focal point for issues that should be worked out independently of economics.

Elsewhere in this book we talk about working on a relationship almost as if it were a separate entity—nurturing it as we would if it were an independent being with a life of its own. This perspective is quite applicable when dealing with joint finances. Nurturing our relationship with regard to money entails talking through and developing appropriate financial plans with our partner, continually reassessing and updating those plans, and establishing a clear understanding of our respective areas of financial authority and responsibility.

I once read about a marriage ceremony that involves the symbolic lighting of three candles—one for each of the partners and a third for the relationship itself. An important point about the ceremony is that the candles representing each of the partners are left lit, rather than being snuffed out in order to leave just one single candle. This, I feel, symbolizes very clearly the desirability of both people maintaining their individuality and to some degree their independence, yet each contributing to the building of the relationship. This balance between individuality and shared effort seems more relevant and appropriate today than ever before.

10

Fostering Intimacy and Staying Connected

I. Charles Thomas Cayce

I think it's safe to say that most couples enjoy the feeling of being closely connected to another person in an intimate relationship. But a feeling of closeness in a relationship waxes and wanes. It is often hard to sustain consistently. Like many couples, Leslie and I have gone through periods when we haven't felt very closely connected with each other. In some instances these periods of feeling more distant have lasted months. (Leslie writes about such "dry spells" later in this chapter.)

Over the past few years we've adopted several ways in which we've tried to enhance our feeling of connectedness.

119

One of the most important ways of building our sense of intimacy is simply *spending time alone together.* We take trips together. We once set aside Saturday mornings to be together, and Tuesday evenings for going out together, as special times of being close with each other.

But for some reason we still run into intervals when we seem to have less time alone. Other demands pour in on us and distract us. And even when we do find time to be alone, we can still end up feeling somehow distant from each other.

This brings up a few questions that I believe are important to a lot of people in relationships: What comprises that feeling of connectedness? What's it made up of? How can it be nurtured, other than by simply spending time alone together?

Just being in physical proximity with your chosen partner is a start, of course. But as Leslie and I have found out, by itself, it's not enough to guarantee connectedness. You can live in the same house with someone, eat meals together, and spend a lot of time in close physical proximity with that person and yet still feel a lack of connectedness and intimacy with him or her.

One of the things that I think is most important in giving depth to the sense of intimacy between two people is *sharing experiences together.* Different types of shared experiences would, no doubt, work best for different couples, and each twosome would probably want to partake in a variety of activities together. The important thing is that both people participate and be as fully engaged in the experience as possible.

Sometimes this sharing can involve just the two people themselves. This is the type of connectedness-building activity that my wife and I are taking part in when we go out together for breakfast or dinner.

At other times, *more people can be included.* I've often

felt a special closeness with Leslie when the two of us were out together with other relatives or friends. Going to a party together, attending a movie with a larger group, and working together as part of a team are just a few examples of the many different group activities that can enhance a couple's sense of connectedness.

Sharing feelings is often a very effective way of fostering intimacy. It's important that our communication be about not just superficial things, but things that really matter to each of us. Honesty in expressing our feelings is essential. Leslie and I enjoy sharing our deeper emotions and reactions whenever we're in a place that we both find appealing, whether it's in traveling through a foreign country, paddling a canoe together, or simply working in our garden.

Sharing sexual experiences and feelings can greatly help build the sense of connectedness between a man and a woman. For a lot of couples this is probably the most powerful way of all to strengthen intimacy. For one thing, two people can be brought closer together by just touching each other. This is one area that often slips out of a relationship, somehow getting squeezed from the daily routine. Though there are exceptions, there is typically an inverse relationship between the length of time a man and a woman have been together and the amount of touching they do. The longer their involvement endures, the less attention is paid to touching. Giving touch the importance it deserves seems to be particularly a problem for men, and it can take a bit of effort to make sure that this form of communication doesn't get overlooked in the relationship.

I feel that many couples would find it worthwhile to monitor the *amount of touching* they engage in. You and your partner might want to try taking a look together at the past week or so and adding up the amount of time spent in direct physical contact. The next step would be to work on increasing your total touching time over the following week and to look at any effects this has on your relationship.

The Edgar Cayce readings contain quite a bit of material on touch and the exchange of energy and healing that it can bring about. Dolores Krieger, a nurse in New York City, has done some fascinating research into this subject. The indication is that touch can be of definite physical benefit to people, and from time to time I've talked with my doctor about the importance of touching. I believe that the healing effect of touch works on the emotional level as well as on the physical, and that touching can add to the intimacy of any relationship.

Sharing experiences, feelings, sexual activity, and touch all can enhance the closeness two people feel for each other. Yet, as Leslie and I have discovered during our more distant periods, building connectedness is not a matter of formula or technique. We can be engaged in one or all of those forms of sharing, we can be together in a special place doing something we both enjoy doing, and still there will be times when the intimacy we're seeking just doesn't happen. This usually indicates that in some way we have failed to engage ourselves in our common activity. It could be that one or both of us is distracted by outside concerns. Perhaps we need to look for new ways of adding to our feeling of intimacy with each other, or maybe we just need to try different combinations of the ones we already know about.

Distractions from personal sharing can come in a wide variety of forms. Two that get to me most frequently involve stressful situations at work and concern over the health or welfare of someone I care about. I am inclined to avoid talking about these outside threats to intimacy, and thus I tend to tighten up and draw into myself. I imagine that a lot of men and women react in the same way. This can create a kind of mutual withdrawal between two partners that snowballs and feeds upon itself. Each person senses the withdrawal in the other, and each responds by withdrawing further into himself or herself. Or when one withdraws, the other person may become anxious and pursue the one withdrawing, making unwelcome demands.

In thinking of couples who have close relationships I admire and respect, I've been struck by their ability to *work through difficult times together.* They're willing to share their feelings during periods of increased distance. From what they've told me and what I myself have observed, they often come out of these periods with a renewed and increased sense of connectedness. This ability seems to me to be a very healthy part of their relationships.

Yet I find that I have a certain hesitancy to do the same thing myself. My reluctance to share my personal concerns with my partner during the distant times might stem from a feeling that doing so could make me more vulnerable, or perhaps I'm just too proud to admit to my worries. Part of the cause is my underlying inclination to avoid the unpleasantness of talking about anything negative; I'd rather focus on the positive and put more energy into that. I'm concerned that talking about the negative will add to the stress by drawing me more deeply into the situation mentally and accentuating the pain.

But in spite of my uneasiness, I invariably find that when I do talk about these stresses with Leslie, we end up feeling closer. I feel closer to her, and she says that she feels closer to me. Discussing my concerns with her doesn't create more stress for me; it creates less. More often than not, she's able to offer observations and insights that are helpful to me in resolving the stress.

Another important lesson that Leslie and I are learning from our distant periods is that *it's OK to accept these intervals.* We don't have to get angry when we find ourselves going through a phase where we're distracted and not feeling as much connectedness as we would like. We don't have to panic and try to force a sense of intimacy that just isn't there at the moment. And we—perhaps for this one I should say I—don't have to avoid talking about it for fear of upsetting the other person. We can discuss our more withdrawn times without either of us getting upset.

Accepting these periods of reduced intimacy doesn't mean that we've resigned ourselves to mediocrity in our relationship. We haven't lowered our expectations of what we want in terms of connectedness. We've just come to accept the fact that relationships go through different phases, and it's OK if some of these phases involve a less intense feeling of connectedness than others.

This point is illustrated by a progression that's common to an awful lot of relationships. When two people first hook up with each other, they're likely to experience a honeymoon-type period of ardent infatuation. This is the stage of passionate attraction that's shown so often in the movies. On one level, most of us realize that this phase doesn't last forever. Yet, when we recognize that our relationship has reached the end of the honeymoon, it can be quite difficult to face. Some of us may react by trying anything we can think of to make this period go on and on. But to me it seems much more realistic and helpful to accept the close of the infatuation stage and to see what new dimensions of love develop as the relationship matures.

For the truth is that almost all relationships do move beyond the time of passionate attraction. Periods of distraction do follow. They might not be the ideal, but they have their place and they're OK. This kind of acceptance feels good to me. In some ways, the distance phases have even helped Leslie and me to feel closer to each other. It's reassuring to look at someone you love and say, "Yes, we have had closer times than this, and we'll have them again, and that's all right." It's also very reassuring to know that your partner understands.

For us, a final important aspect of staying connected has

to do with humor. Our ability to step back and laugh at ourselves, to find the humor in our lives, and to laugh together can build and heal in a special way. For example, when traveling we often have tensions and calamities that could pull us apart. However, as a family we enjoy quickly turning these experiences into comical scenes; even playing "charades": one person acts out an experience we had (usually a more trying one) and the others guess which one it was. We end up laughing at ourselves in no time, and in the process the earlier tensions dissipate.

II. Leslie Goodman Cayce

Less obvious, perhaps, but equally critical periods occur as "dry spells" between partners. Like tidal actions, these occur naturally in a long-term relationship and sometimes in a brief one. These ebb tides of feeling often are insidiously invisible. They creep up silently until one or both partners realize "the cold war" is on, as a friend of mine says. Such low periods may include minimal communication beyond perfunctories and necessities; a lull in caring (inertia) or in the desire to change; minimal physical touching and affection; a feeling of impatience; a sense that one or both are changing, accompanied by a vague dread of being left out or behind; feeling depressed, critical, bored, restless, distracted, or preoccupied.

The dry spell in a relationship is a common occurrence. It varies only in degrees and in the unique tolerance level each partner has for these dry spells.

Marriage, beyond the honeymoon phase, holds some well-defined dry spells, defined by Gail Sheehy as "passages," such as the seven-year itch. The seven- (or any) year itch is truly a classic dry spell. It implies boredom, the loss of sparkle, when all the petty irritations of living with someone loom large. It often seems to be predominantly a state

of mind, a pitfall that can emerge at any time. Looking outside the marriage for a surrogate substitute partner at these
times is, to my mind, ultimately wasteful. It is here that a
dry spell may become a crisis or critical period, instigating
major outer turmoil (i.e., a threat or reality of changing partners). If so, it prolongs or postpones a necessary process:
taking a closer look at oneself, deepening communication
and risk-taking with one's partner, experiencing the break-
throughs to the other side of this dry spell wherein lies a
stronger foundation of love, trust, and commitment. It has
been said elsewhere so much more eloquently that what
we see in our loved ones is a custom-made mirror. When
we dare to peer at this mirror rather than turn away from it,
inevitably there is beauty and richness within.

The symptoms of my dry spells are usually restlessness
and recurring irritations with Charles Thomas. Such feelings are often the cover for a deeper dissatisfaction that
rightfully belongs at home with me, so I have come to regard them as indications of misplaced responsibility. More
often than not, I have slipped into a frame of mind of wanting him to "do it" for me; thus, the misplaced responsibility.
How often this is the case! If I am unhappy with some aspect of myself and my life, I subtly, oh so subtly, put the
blame or onus on Charles Thomas to fix it, to make it better.
Sometimes I see this in quasi-Jungian terms of my masculine side—the impulse to initiate and take charge—is dormant, out to lunch. Needless to say, this can set off a chain
reaction with one's partner who, all on an unspoken level,
often feels an added weight of some sort and resents it, tries
to rebel or throw it off. A downward cycle—another signal
of a dry spell—can quickly ensue. "Downward cycle" means
both parties feel caught in an action-reaction chain that can
be difficult to break away from; e.g., not wanting to take responsibility, I'd sit back and let Charles Thomas make decisions. He'd then resent being the sole initiator, while I'd be

irritated with myself for allowing it in the first place—and the cycle goes on down from there.

Dry spells are often subtle, creeping up gradually. On the one hand, they are to be expected and absorbed in the course of any long-term, close relationship, part of a natural ebb and flow. On the other hand, they are like beacons of potential dangers and we need to pay attention to their frequency and duration. Charles Thomas and I have become more vocal with each other than ever before, verbally acknowledging times that we feel unconnected and distant. It helps us to deflate fears as we embrace these times as "OK" and are not thrown off-balance by them with thoughts like "There must be something wrong with us if . . . " (sounds like an old societal or childhood tape). Perhaps we are learning to see the ebbs (stumbling blocks) as messengers (stepping-stones) pointing toward areas needing growth or renewal.

For Charles Thomas and me silence can serve as an easy way to avoid conflict. We both opt first to "let it pass," if at all possible. The catch is to make sure that letting it pass doesn't really mean letting it fester. Also, if I let it pass too much, things do start to feel dry and lifeless between us. The readings often advised couples: Don't be angry at the same time. We like that. This past year I have consciously chosen not to let things pass sometimes, even if there are good reasons to. ("Bad timing/he's tired/the children are around/I'm tired/ it's petty/I've said it before.") More than once I have run out to catch his car about to head for work in the morning and hashed something out in the yard in my pajamas. Or I've called him in the middle of the day to try to settle something. So here again there is a need for balance. After years together we are still discovering "new" (for us) ways of responding to dry spells and critical periods. This, to me, is the trial and error of implementing, living out the readings' admonition to find the answer within and that "this may best be answered within self."

A useful response to a dry spell, we have found, is to review ideals. The ideals list reminds us, at a time when we've often forgotten, of things we love to do and want to do or of attitudes we want to strengthen. When I have lost my bearings and feel confused, it is centering to turn my attention to ideals or to rework them. Sometimes, during times of confusion, adding or changing mental and physical ideals feels good and right because then the list seems more real, more truly a reflection of all of me—the weak with the strong, the troubled with the calm.

Our somewhat intuitive response has been more in line with the biblical saying, "For everything there is a season . . . " (Eccles. 3:1) "A time for dry spells" would sum up our response. This is distinct from avoiding acknowledgment and is different from denial. It is not a "running from" as much as it is an "embracing of." In Buddhist terms, it is affirming through non-action.

Sometimes an outer circumstance initiates a critical period. In November of 1987, without warning, I had a miscarriage at twelve weeks of pregnancy. My shock soon turned into a desolate feeling of emptiness. An immediate result of the miscarriage for me was a plunge into a dry spell. The emptiness I felt was profound. I withdrew and felt little else for weeks. I'd been knocked off my feet. I felt and saw the fragility of life, the swift surprise element of bodily malfunction, the feeling of helplessness, and the lack of control triggered by helplessness. The miscarriage was clearly a catalyst for me to look at myself and the direction of my life with eyes and a lens that are different from before the miscarriage.

I don't recall expressing these feelings often with Charles Thomas. There didn't seem to be much purpose in sharing; it didn't relieve or release. I did take time to be alone and to listen, just to be with myself. I held the belief—before and during this time—that everything is purposeful and that I was listening for purposes. The readings say so often in different ways that everything, every meeting, happens for a purpose.

Charles Thomas and I already had two beautiful daughters, who were then four and six years old. In my lonely exploration through sadness and disappointment over the miscarriage I saw that another baby may have been a way of postponing or avoiding taking responsibility for certain voids in my life. Added years of child care would have afforded me a temporary escape from a hard, ambiguous task I had sensed for many years, increasing certain elements—like spirituality and a career—in my life.

Sensing a deeper meaning behind my pregnancy and prospective parenthood, I was then faced with the task of deciphering possible purposes of miscarrying, the loss of the promise. I saw it as an indication to put up the mantle, to begin the move on from procreating to focus on our two children. Above all, I felt called to feel God's presence in the midst of the loss and the lack of understanding, to believe in the rightness of it every step of the way, and to continue looking for lessons.

Charles Thomas was sensitive enough not to push me to be engaged during this reflective time. My grief, with its sadness, anger, and finally healing, needed to run its course. Even now our older daughter infrequently asks, "How old would our baby be now?" Perhaps it is one of her ways of still working out the loss.

I am thankful that Charles Thomas was open, yet let me be. One of the ways we found we were enabled to take an accepting, embracing stance during this personal critical time was to accept it all—the silence and the quiet sharing. It's the opposite of panic. Major decisions are avoided (major anything is to be avoided). When I look back upon those months, I recall them as very quiet.

I was listening, looking for a sense of purpose within the loss, for lessons to be learned, insights to be gained. Yet all the while I tried to honor the instinctual, emotional responses as they surfaced. Critical periods (and/or dry spells) call forth a juggling between accepting the present ebb or intensity and, on the other hand, upholding the ideal/philosophy that life is purposeful—ever or especially during the dark times. If it is true that our minds have great potential and ability to create, then these periods can also be powerful opportunities to think and pray about healing.

Culturally we are quite encouraged to do something about critical periods and/or dry spells. It is implicit—sometimes explicit—that they "should" (aha!) not occur or "should" not last too long. Most of us can tolerate only so much stress, but it seems that critical times naturally occur in cycles. Seen as times of potential healing, they need not be avoided, dreaded, or gotten through as quickly as possible. They can be accepted as part of a relationship's life cycle. They can be seen as calls toward new growth.

Probably the most common response to dry spells is the "ostrich" response. Pay minimal attention. Don't think about it. Don't talk about it. If it's uncomfortable, threatening, or unsettling, pretend it doesn't exist. Keep busy and it'll go away. The ostrich response can be a distortion of "focus on the positive," for it is not positive. Sometimes it may work. If two people agree to this response, they are also implicitly agreeing to a lot of denial and distance, a lack of intimacy in their relationship.

Another response to times of stress or emptiness is the one I had after my miscarriage: It is to face what surfaces, acknowledge any feelings—fears, doubts, disappointment—and then wait. No action is required. For me, contained within the silence of waiting were prayers, prayers simply for guidance that I might see whatever lessons or opportunities were hidden within that experience, and to be open, to trust in a purposefulness still unraveling and in an ongoing, healing process.

Another response encouraged in the Cayce readings is that of giving. "Dare to speak gently, when even thine self is troubled." (694-2) If the crisis is between two people, giving means open, honest sharing. It means taking the risk of showing (giving) one's deep, true feelings. With an individual, giving can be in simple acts of kindness and thoughtfulness.

During dry spells or crises it helps to remember that the readings repeatedly say that we are never given more than we can handle. That, coupled with the notion that everything that happens is purposeful, has often helped me through these difficult periods.

11

꧁꧂

Sex and the
Oneness of All Energy

*T*he central point of the Edgar Cayce readings on sex is that sexual energy is a manifestation of the one force, the creative force of God. As such, the readings consistently stress the beauty of sex, as opposed to the prudish Victorian view of sex as sin.

The readings explain that there are endocrine centers in the body which serve as the focal points through which spiritual energy becomes manifested in the physical. There are seven of these centers that are a special focus of the Cayce readings and related materials on this subject. The gonad center is the first of the seven. This doesn't mean that the gonads are the ultimate source of the energy, for, being spiritual, it is nonphysical in origin. But the gonad center is the starting point of the energy's manifestation in the body. From there, the energy moves through the other six centers, to be disseminated throughout the entire physical being.

Some authors have taken the view that sexual expression is limited to the lower endocrine centers. The implication is that the proper way of utilizing this energy is to sublimate it, raise it to the higher centers, and use it in ways other than sexual activity.

The Edgar Cayce readings do not support this concept that sex is an inferior use of spiritual energy. The readings offer a more unified perspective of the creative force. There's no dichotomy here, no implication that sex is negative and involves only the lower centers, while spirituality is positive and concerns the higher ones. Rather, creative energy is seen as the one unified force of God, and sex is one vehicle through which two people can use this energy to express love together. It is a good and appropriate part of a relationship when it's used in a creative act of manifesting God in our lives.

The readings' portrayal of sex as a manifestation of the God force in us is something a lot of people have trouble accepting. Some may reject this concept because they have difficulty associating sex with God. At times, I, despite the guidance in the Cayce material, dissociate sex from spirituality in my own mind.

Like many people, I have a tendency to mentally connect spirituality with a lack of sexuality. This is probably the result of conditioning during my childhood experiences in church, which had nothing to do with sex. The images which I typically associated with spirituality, such as celibate religious leaders (nuns and priests), contained no hint of sexuality. Part of me still feels that spirituality is asexual, that sex belongs in the irreverent world of *Playboy* maga-

zine, singles bars, and illicit activities, and that these two
worlds are very far apart. The Cayce readings reject this less-
than-ideal view of sex, but it's one that I'm afraid many of us
are at least influenced by.

One of the reasons for this influence, I think, is our
society's inconsistent and somewhat odd attitude toward
sex. On the one hand, sex pervades our advertising and our
culture in a very superficial way. At the same time, it is not
really discussed maturely or constructively. There's a long-
standing controversy over sex education in our public
schools, in which some parents oppose it entirely. In most
families and even between adults, the subject isn't generally discussed with care or with a healthy perspective. Psy-
chotherapists tell us that feelings of sexual energy are
present in childhood, but most parents tend to disregard or
try to stifle these feelings in their children. There's a lack of
serious communication about both the philosophical and
the physiological aspects of sexuality.

The Cayce readings, mindful of the resultant gaps in our
knowledge of sex, suggested the basic importance of
studying *Gray's Anatomy,* a classic textbook. This is a simple
measure that can help anyone gain a fundamental understanding of the body. The readings recommend that we start
helping our children reach such an understanding at a very
early age. As adults, we can work on developing an appreciation of the beauty of the body and a knowledge of how it
works—both our own body and that of our partner's.

Somehow there's a hesitancy to undertake this type of
study. I've felt this reluctance in myself. It seems to be based
on an apprehension that looking at sex in this clinical way
might take some of the beauty and mystery out of it. I'm
sure that this kind of examination of sex doesn't necessarily
have to have that effect.

There are, of course, a few books that do take a factual
approach to sexuality; the Kinsey reports come to mind as

one example. But even these works cannot take the place of honest communication among family members and sexual partners. Again, I find myself falling into the cultural pattern of not talking or thinking about the more meaningful aspects of sexuality very often.

The way sex is portrayed in some of our media—in advertising and romantic television programs with their bedroom scenes—can't help us reach a sound understanding of the proper role of sexuality. Unless we're careful, these sources can create a confusing image of the sexual experience, one that I think men would be especially susceptible to. There's a discrepancy between these images of what sex or the ideal sexual partner should be like and the ones presented elsewhere in our culture. This inconsistency can create conflict and confusion for us, both in our conscious minds and at deeper levels within us.

As a way of resolving this conflict, it would be worthwhile to think through or to talk through what our ideal sexual partner and experience would be like. For me, and I think for a lot of us, what we come up with is likely to be quite different from the image created by our culture.

We might bear in mind that sex is just one facet of a relationship. It's given a lot of weight in our society, and it is sometimes pictured as being all-important and completely indicative of what's going on between two people at other levels. Actually, though, the place sex should have in any relationship is totally up to the individuals involved. If a man and a woman agree that sex is going to play a big part in their life together, that's fine for them. There's no right or wrong about the degree of importance of sex.

I feel that in assessing the significance of sex in a relationship, we must adopt a balanced point of view. Sex is neither all-important nor trivial. It does have a depth to it that we shouldn't minimize, and its implications tend to be more profound than those of other parts of a relationship.

There's a deep mystery to sex, not in a superficial aura of secrecy imposed by society, but in the sense of something that challenges human understanding.

While Westerners haven't explored this aspect of sex very seriously, various Eastern religions certainly suggest that the mystery is there and that it relates to self-understanding and spiritual growth. The Indian philosophy of tantric yoga, for example, is greatly concerned with combining spirituality and sexuality. Such schools of thought don't view the proper role of sex as being related to just the lower endocrine centers; it is considered part of a total process of spiritual development.

There are other alternatives to the typically asexual Christian view of spirituality. In Judaism, for instance, there is a tradition by which a man and his wife bring in the Sabbath by making love on Friday evening. Sexual activity is seen as holy and an integrative part of the peace and joy of the Sabbath. There's a feeling of oneness between sex and spirituality, as opposed to the distinction some denominations make between what is good and of God, and what is sexual and base.

Both the Eastern and the Jewish traditions appear to be compatible with the Edgar Cayce readings' view that sex is to be used to express the creative force of God in our lives. Though the readings don't really go into the specifics of how to combine sex and spirituality, they do say that this is the way sexual energy should be used.

From the perspective of the Cayce material, there's more to sex than we usually assume. Sex is a form of energy whose applications are much broader than sexual activity. It can be used to create and express love in our lives and help us build loving attitudes within ourselves.

In the readings, I get the impression that the ideal in relation to sexuality has to do with our existence as incomplete beings. Sexual union with someone we love can give us a taste of the oneness we can experience with a God we love. In this way, our sexual seeking is a microcosm reflecting the total quest of our souls.

In Jungian terms, we're searching for a union within ourselves, a knowledge of our true selves. When we relate to a partner who in a lot of ways represents parts of us that are as yet untapped, a oneness or a wholeness occurs. On the physical level the oneness comes through the sexual union. It can happen on the mental and spiritual levels as well. Sometimes the union occurs on all three planes at once. This represents a kind of ultimate experience, one that makes sexual activity really holy. It gives us a glimpse of what our union with God will be like.

In order to achieve this physical, mental, and spiritual oneness, it's necessary for a couple to feel open toward each other on all three levels. During sex, our boundaries are penetrated, both literally and figuratively, and no longer fulfill their normal, everyday functions. Our defenses are down. Two people are in a more open position when they're making love than in almost any other situation. Our potential for achieving true union with our partner is greater the more willing and ready we are for that openness. Putting on the brakes can only hinder it.

If we are prepared to let our boundaries down and merge, one of the things that happens on the physical level is that the distinction between our gratification and our partner's gets fuzzy. It can become hard to tell whether we're focusing on ourselves or on the other person. It seems that there's a point somewhere in between where we're not focusing exclusively on either one. We're simply open, in terms of both being gratified and giving gratification. The distinction between the two loses its clarity as we merge.

One thing that can make this physical openness during sex easier to achieve is honest communication between the two partners. This can be quite a challenge for some people, because verbalizing what pleases us and what doesn't makes us extremely vulnerable. For many, it's easier just not to talk about it.

Men are particularly prone to becoming defensive in these discussions of how to give sexual pleasure. Such comments from one's partner can be inappropriately interpreted as criticism of technique or performance. Avoiding this type of defensiveness requires care, both in expressing these remarks sensitively and in receiving them freely without taking offense.

One area in which I have found such communication to be very helpful concerns the preludes to sexual activity. There seems to be a considerable man/woman difference here. Lead-ins, such as dinner, dancing, and setting up a romantic situation, are likely to be much more important to a woman than to a man. While I'm aware of this particular difference between the sexes, it's helpful to me when Leslie reminds me that the preludes are a more closely connected part of sexual activity for her than they are for me.

Openness in the sexual aspect of a relationship involves mental as well as physical participation. When a person enters into sexual activity, the mental attitude can be geared in a variety of ways. If we want to share a union with our partner on the mental level, we'll pay some attention to our attitudes, doing what we can to adopt ones that are compatible with the oneness we're seeking. This can involve, for example, using the mind to heighten our feelings of gentleness and kindness toward our partner and expressing these attitudes within the sexual act.

For the experience of oneness between two people to be total, their openness to each other must also extend to the spiritual level. If we're prepared for this complete oneness, one step we can take to help it come about is to invite into our sexual activity a deeper awareness of our partner, through prayer. In so doing, we can be working with a form of selflessness. Through prayer and visualization, a man and a woman can openly acknowledge that they're both about to enter a more receptive state; they can endeavor to heighten their awareness of one another; and they can build upon this receptivity and openness, increasing their sense of union with each other.

Leslie and I have spoken with couples who've prayed and gone through a ritual together before having intercourse. This practice has a fine potential for expressing the creative energy of the spirit through sex. It can be a powerful way of achieving the deepest possible union with one's partner, using the single creative force to build love in our lives and receiving through sexual activity a foretaste of the oneness we will experience with God.

Sex and Intimacy: Sexual Choices

The choices we make as we engage in sexual activity are an intense microcosm of our decisions in the total area of spiritual growth. In every aspect of life, our fundamental choice is whether to manifest God's infinite love for all or to act in our own limited self-interest. In sex, one alternative is to focus on lovemaking in a self-centered way. There's certainly a strong physical drive to concentrate on our own gratification, especially once we become aroused and caught up in the culmination of a sexual encounter.

Our other alternative is to move beyond preoccupation with self-gratification and connect with the other person. This involves becoming aware of our partner's needs and doing what we can to satisfy them. I'm not referring simply to physical pleasure and orgasm here. Our love for our partner has to take account of his or her emotional, mental, and spiritual needs as well. In this way we can build a joint positive experience with our loved one that unites and fulfills us on all levels of our being.

I must admit that, for me anyway, this concept is a bit idealized. At times I find it hard to bridge the giving and the receiving aspects of sex. The very intensity of the sexual experience tends to make us focus on our own gratification or on that of our partner's. There's a tendency to feel that we have to give up something of our own pleasure if we're going to do our best to please the other person.

Sex need not be an either/or proposition, however. There can be deep joy in giving, particularly to a partner we love. As an example, in giving a Christmas present to a child, we find that there is a very real, tangible pleasure in experiencing the happiness of another person as he or she receives the gift. We don't have to be getting the present ourselves to feel the happiness, and we don't have to sacrifice any of our own joy to do the giving. In a similar way, sex can enable us to experience true joy in selflessness.

Our basic choice regarding sex is whether to use it creatively in this way or to engage in it merely for the sake of self-indulgence. It seems that Cayce was consciously aware of these alternatives faced by each of us as we go about sorting out our use of sexual energy and our relationships with others. In a letter that he wrote to a person who had received a series of readings from him, he warned of the possibly self-destructive effects of misusing his creative power: "[Sex] is the line between the great and the vagabond, the good and the bad . . . [If it is] allowed to run wild to self-indulgence, [it] becomes physical and mental derangement."

Further, he emphasized the potential godliness of sex if its energy is applied constructively: "[Sex] is the expression of creative life in the earth. But if we lose sight that it's an expression of God and accredit it to something else, we deny the very promises that God has made to us all."

As we make our day-to-day decisions concerning the role of sex in our lives, it would be good to be aware of the influence exerted by memory patterns at the endocrine-gland level. In any area of life, each decision we make builds a pattern of action. These patterns—we might also think of them as habits—are stored as memory in the body's endocrine centers. They are stimulated whenever we confront a similar decision. In other words, every choice we make is influenced by our unconscious record of how we have reacted to similar situations in the past.

Some of these memory patterns have been created by our decisions earlier in the current lifetime. Others have arisen from our actions during previous incarnations. Each of the endocrine-gland centers bears the patterns related to a particular aspect of life. For example, the patterns at the center associated with the solar plexus and the adrenal glands concern how we have used power in the past. Those stored in the heart center relate to love and sharing, like that between parent and child. And the memory patterns created by our past actions in regard to sex are connected primarily with the endocrine centers of the reproductive glands.

As an illustration of how these patterns from the past can affect our present decisions, let's consider how a man might act toward women other than his wife. In his relations with other women, he might have the choice of indulging himself mentally or physically. Perhaps in previous incarnations and the earlier years of his present life, he has created a pattern of sexual self-indulgence. If so, he could be left with a strong predisposition to behave in the same way at present. Whether his past actions involved the same women he is meeting now or different ones, the patterns will be stimulated when he faces those same choices again. Unless he's careful, he might find himself influenced to act in ways that will have a negative effect on his relationship with his wife and on his associations with the other women. The more aware each of us is of the effect of our own memory patterns, the more likely we'll choose constructive actions in regard to sex and in every other area of life.

There's one important point of clarification that I feel should be made. Using sexual energy creatively does not necessarily mean using it in other than sexual ways. It's true that this force can be directed into creative nonsexual efforts—it can be sublimated, in other words—and some people suggest that this is the superior way to use it. But I've never found this concept in the Cayce readings. When Cayce's letter speaks of sex as "the line between the great and the vagabond," he's not saying that in order to be great one must abstain from sex and channel the energy into creating beautiful paintings or music; and he's not saying that using the life force sexually makes a person a vagabond.

What the Cayce readings warned against is using the energy self-indulgently. To me, sexual self-indulgence means mentally and physically taking the energy too lightly. It means playing with it. There is power in sexual energy and a connection to the one higher force. We are called to recognize its power and that force in our lives and treat it with great respect. Sexual self-indulgence, then, is not a question of whether or how often we have sex. The deciding factor is the attitude with which we use this energy.

Speaking of avoiding self-indulgence, a gut-level issue for many people is the belief that real sexual enjoyment needs to have an element of lust and abandonment, of passion. In part, this is a culturally created myth, but it's one that affects a lot of us, including me. At times I feel a little uneasy when reviewing the Cayce readings on sex, for it is possible to interpret some of them as implying that we need to remove those qualities of passion from sex in order to make it more selfless. My concern is that in taking passion out of our sexual activity we may de-energize the experience in some way.

In terms of the endocrine glands, the gonad center is the starting point of sexual energy in the body. It seems that when having a sexual experience we can keep the energy focused in the gonads, which to me implies lust and abandonment; or we can move it upward through the other centers, which I mentally associate with making our sexual activity more selfless. There's some kind of conditioning in me saying that if we move that energy from the gonad center, we somehow diminish the total pleasure of the experience.

A closer reading of the Edgar Cayce material, however, shows that this source does not equate passion with self-indulgence. Nothing in the readings says that getting caught up in the sexual experience with abandon is bad or wrong or not of God. There's no essential conflict between passion and the selfless use of sex, and so there's no reason to think that if we're feeling passion, we're not experiencing sex as we should.

The key to combining passionate sex with selfless sex is love. With love, the distinction between the two falls away. As long as we feel loving toward our partner, our sexual activity builds love in both our lives. This makes our sexual experiences together spiritual and divinely creative, no matter how passionate they may be.

It has been said that the degree to which our society is preoccupied with sexuality indicates how many of us are looking for sexual experiences. I take this search to be a bright and hopeful sign. It shows that people sense a need for wholeness and deeper communication in their lives.

There is more to sex than the exchange of energy. There is a mystery, hinted at in Eastern literature, that extends far beyond the physical. The sex drive can be used to move to a deeper level of communication and commitment among people. Thus, our search for sexual expression can be a stepping-stone to a more creative and fulfilling life.

An important point is that there is no ultimate in our exploration of sexual energy. Realizing this could save a lot of us from being let down. Before most people ever engage in sexual activity, they form expectations of what sex is going to be like. With these expectations they create a highly idealized fantasy. They invariably find that their first sexual experience, whenever it happens, is disappointing. The reality doesn't measure up to the fantasy.

To a large degree, this disappointment comes about because the people were expecting sex to be ideal, to match their fantasy. But there is no ideal sex act or sexual partner. It's just not possible to discover a secret or a magic formula that will ensure perfect sex, the perfect sexual technique, or the perfect relationship. No matter how fulfilling our experience of sexuality may be, there will always be further developments awaiting us.

What we have is a continual path of exploration and discovery, an ongoing process of growth and understanding. For many of us, our progress along that path is likely to be gradual. We're faced with the exciting challenge to be as honest and loving in our relationships as we can be, so that our sexuality will be a source of creativity and spiritual development throughout our lives. With each other it seems to me that our sexual relationship has gone through the same growth process, including the periods of tension and separateness, that has been true for our relationship as a whole. An important insight for me has been that this aspect of our relationship can be talked about, worked on, and developed just as with other parts of our lives.

Part IV

Understanding
and Strengthening
Love Relationships
— Charles Thomas Cayce —

12

Understanding Relationships Through Dreams

One valuable source of information about our intimate relationships that is often ignored or not understood is our dreams. Whether we always remember them or not, most of us occasionally have dreams concerning our partners and other loved ones. The messages in these dreams can be an aid to better understanding one another and working through unresolved issues.

Edgar Cayce gave over 600 readings to interpret dreams presented to him. Many of these dream interpretations focused on the personal relationships of the dreamer and helped the dreamer understand them better. My own expe-

147

rience with dreams demonstrates that they can furnish valuable assistance in enabling us to draw closer to each other.

Perhaps a large part of the reason for this has to do with the nature of both relationships and dreams. In most of our close relationships, communication and interaction go beyond the intellectual, rational level of the mind. It reaches the energies and feelings in the deepest parts of ourselves.

Like relationships, dreams seem to reflect energies and feelings beyond the intellect. The Cayce readings speak of dreams as connecting the body and the conscious mind with the deeper levels of our being. As one reading on sleep and dreaming expressed it, " . . . when the physical consciousness is at rest, the other self communes with the *soul* of the body . . . " (5754-2) Many of our dreams result from this subconscious communion with our own souls. Thus, they are a prime vehicle for relaying to the conscious mind material about ourselves that we might not otherwise be aware of. For a good number of us, much of this material will concern our relationships.

The psychotherapist, Carl Jung, tells of a conversation he had that illustrates the extent to which most of us in the modern Western world tend to limit ourselves to operating from the conscious mind. Jung was exploring with Ochwiay Biano, a Pueblo Indian chief, the differences between his people and the white man.

Biano said that white people always seemed restless and uneasy, always searching. Jung asked why the chief thought the white man might be this way. The chief replied that it was because white people thought with their heads, and it was well known among his people that this was not the proper way to think. Jung asked how Indians thought, and the chief replied that they thought with the heart.

It may well be that part of the reason we struggle with so many of our relationships is that some of us think only with our heads; we are not enough aware of our own deeper levels. These deeper aspects of our being are precisely the ones that dreams are so well suited to helping us reach. An episode in *The Little Prince*, one of my father's favorite books and also one of mine, shows the importance of getting beyond the intellect. There's a special conversation between the Little Prince and a fox at the end of their visit:

" 'Good-bye,' said the fox. 'And now here is my secret. A very simple secret: It is only with the heart that one can see rightly; what is essential is invisible to the eye.'

" 'What is essential is invisible to the eye,' the Little Prince repeated so that he would be sure to remember."

Seeing with the heart can show us much that is invisible to the eye. Dreams have sometimes been described as a language of the heart. Because relationships so often involve the heart, dreams can provide important insights into this aspect of our lives.

In spite of the tremendous amount of understanding our dreams offer us, many of us have trouble recalling them. Though remembering our dreams can be hard, their potential helpfulness makes the effort well worthwhile. There are several techniques that can help make dream recall easier. Here are a few that often prove useful in this endeavor:

1. Keep a notebook and a pencil beside your bed and record each dream as soon after waking as possible.

2. Suggest to yourself every night as you fall asleep, "I will remember my dreams."

3. If you wake up during the night, pick up the pencil and see if you can recall and write down dream fragments. Do the same in the morning upon awakening, even if you don't feel that you remember a dream. Sometimes just picking up the pencil and putting it to the paper will stimulate recall.

Even after we have recalled a dream, it can frequently be hard for us to grasp its meaning. One major difficulty affecting both recall and interpretation of dreams has to do with the unpleasant pictures we often paint in them. When dreams show us something about ourselves we don't want to see, a lot of us tend to tune them out. Erich Fromm makes this point quite vividly in his book, *The Forgotten Language:*
" . . . if all our dreams were pleasant . . . in which our hearts' wishes were fulfilled, we might feel friendlier toward them. But many of them leave us in an anxious mood; often they're nightmares from which we awake gratefully acknowledging that we only dreamed. Others, though not nightmares, are disturbing for other reasons. They do not fit the person we are sure we are during daytime. We dream of hating people whom we believe we are fond of, of loving someone whom we thought we had no interest in. We dream of being ambitious, when we are convinced of being modest; we dream of bowing down and submitting when we are so proud of our independence. But worst of all is the fact that we do not understand our dreams while we, the waking person, are sure we can understand anything if we put our minds to it. Rather than be confronted with such an overwhelming proof of the limitations of our understanding, we accuse the dreams of not making sense."

Despite the difficulties sometimes presented in our dreams, their messages can help us in all areas of life, including our relationships. How valuable this assistance will actually prove to be depends upon our purpose in working with our dreams and our willingness to use the insight they provide. Over and over again the Cayce readings stressed the necessity of applying the lessons we have received. As one person was admonished:

> Hence the warning: Make practical all such dreams in the material experiences with others. And know that

if they do not produce creative influences and better associations in thy home, in thy relationships with thy fellow men, something is wrong with same! (2419-1)

If we are truly motivated to understand ourselves and our relationships better and to grow in those relationships, dreams can furnish some very helpful perspectives. I myself have personally benefited from this type of aid. As I was working out my attitude toward marriage and clarifying my feelings about the person whom I would eventually marry, two dreams provided crucial insights.

The first took place during a time when I was struggling with the questions of whether to get married and how to find the right person. I was in my mid-thirties, past the time when most of my friends had married, and I was feeling a lot of pressure to locate a suitable partner and settle down.

I talked often with a close friend, a psychologist who was in the same situation, and we shared our questions and frustrations. I felt like someone on a high diving board who was trying to get up the nerve to jump off. The longer I hesitated, the more difficult it seemed to be.

I was particularly uneasy about finding the right companion and was anxiously searching for her. At the same time, I was trying to work with ideas from the Edgar Cayce readings related to spiritual growth. About that time I had the following dream:

I was with my psychologist friend in a forest clearing. The time period seemed to be the present, yet we were dressed like medieval knights in suits of armor, carrying swords and shields. We were busily polishing our armor. Nearby were our two beautiful, saddled horses. I sensed that we were about to get on our horses and ride out to do our duty as knights—fighting battles, rescuing people in distress, or whatever that duty might have been.

I finished polishing my armor and was having an awk-

ward time trying to mount my horse. My friend gave me a
push. Suddenly my horse started off before I had gained my
balance. He galloped a few steps, and I slipped off into a large
mud puddle. My shining armor that I had spent so long
polishing needed to be polished again! I had to start over!

While sitting on the edge of the puddle cleaning my armor, I recognized the lady for whom I had been searching,
the person who would help me fulfill my mission as a
knight. When she saw herself reflected in the shiny armor
on my chest, which I had just finished repolishing, she
smiled, and we hugged.

In the dream I realized that I didn't need to ride anywhere;
that if I polished my own armor, if I got clear about my own
ideals so that the person who saw me could see herself reflected, I would connect with the lady I was seeking. I realized that seeing aspects of ourselves in each other in this
way is a better process than the frantic riding around and
searching.

This dream provided tremendous relief and was a source
of insight for me at the time. Shortly afterward I met the
woman I had seen in that dream and later we were married.

The second dream gave me important understanding of
my perception of myself in relation to my wife. This dream
occurred a few years before we were married. It was a brief
one and, on the surface, seemed to make no sense.

In the dream, Leslie was walking along a trail in the
woods. The trail was vaguely familiar. It looked like ones that
I had hiked in the mountains of Virginia. As she was walking along the trail, I realized that I was also present in the
dream, but that I was not a person. I was a vine growing
along the ground, and I was not sure that she even noticed
me. I knew what kind of vine I was—a Virginia creeper. I felt
uneasy about our relationship. As a vine, I felt that I wasn't
worthy, and I was afraid she might step on me. End of
dream.

The dream seemed silly at first. But as I talked it over with Leslie, the feelings it brought to the surface became clearer. I found the dream to be a very helpful tool in resolving those feelings and perceptions about myself and our relationship.

This dream illustrates a very important point encountered often in the Edgar Cayce material on dreams involving relationships. The readings almost always interpreted such dreams as comments on the relationships themselves. One major class of dreams, the readings tell us, arises from a subconscious interaction between the dreamer's mind and the minds of the people around the dreamer—"the correlation of mental forces in a physical body to the mental forces of other bodies . . . " (900-13) As a result, many of our dreams can show us aspects of our associations with others that might not be apparent to our conscious minds. This view of dreams is quite different from that of some other schools of thought, which hold that dreams usually concern only the dreamer's life and that other characters in the dream symbolize only the various aspects of the dreamer.

In my own use of dreams as a tool for understanding relationships better, the principle presented in the Cayce readings has usually applied: If the dream involves someone with whom the dreamer has a relationship, begin interpreting it as a commentary about the relationship. My experience has shown this concept to be generally more valid than the alternative approach.

One example of this method of interpretation is given by psychologist Ann Faraday in one of her popular books on dreams. The author tells about a dream she had in which she crept up on her husband while he was sleeping and beat him to death with a carpet sweeper.

She felt that the dream provided a vivid picture of her hostility toward him, which was associated with his attempts to get her to postpone her career and focus on family household responsibilities. The dream helped her recognize the anger she felt in the relationship. The carpet sweeper, of course, was a good symbol for some of her less exciting household duties.

Another method of interpreting this dream would involve asking the dreamer questions, such as, what aspect of herself her husband might symbolize. The dream would then be seen not as a commentary on their relationship, but as perhaps a picture of something happening among different facets of the dreamer herself. According to this view, the dream's message would concern the dreamer's relationship with her husband only indirectly. This, however, is not the approach that is so often suggested in the Cayce readings.

There are several ways in which understanding our dreams can enable us to find greater fulfillment in relationships. Dreams can highlight the positive aspects of our associations, evoking in us appreciation for the good things and encouraging us to build upon them. When things are going less smoothly, they can help us achieve a deeper understanding of the problem areas and point the way toward constructive responses.

Both these possibilities are illustrated in a dream interpretation reading Cayce gave for a man who was working as a stockbroker in partnership with his brother. In the dream, he and his brother were in their office arguing, and it seemed that they were about to dissolve their partnership. This dream highlights the positive potential in their relationship and points out a possible approaching difficulty. The reading identifies its message as follows:

> ... that these [two brothers] are as helpmeets one to another, and that without the strength and the encouragement from the other, *neither* would accomplish that as may be done in unison ...
>
> Then, as the warning—let not that in any manner enter the life that would separate the self from the

abilities of the other, for in this union of strength much may be attained by each. (137-99)

In my own life, dreams have often helped me reach a deeper understanding of my relationships. During that early period when my feelings about my relationship with Leslie were somewhat unresolved, I had a number of meaningful dreams about the two of us. This experience, I believe, reflects the connection between our dreams and our conscious minds. It seems that the more time we spend working on something at the conscious level, the more apt we are to see it as part of our dream lives. As one person who received a great many dream interpretation readings from Cayce was told, "The dreams come as those indications to the entity [the dreamer] of that [which] is held in the mind concerning conditions, surroundings, and such." (900-460)

As I've continued working with my dreams to reach a better understanding of my relationships, they have been valuable in helping me understand aspects of myself that allowed me to have deeper, more meaningful relationships. Dreams have also fostered an awareness of opportunities for creative service with others with whom I have relationships, and they've been a stimulus toward using those opportunities.

They've presented useful memories of possible past-life experiences.

They have given me a better understanding of problems being worked on by others with whom I have relationships.

At times they've warned me of approaching conditions that may be difficult in a relationship, giving me an opportunity to prepare to meet these potential problems. Perhaps a few illustrations of each of these points will provide a clearer idea of some specific ways dreams can be used to enhance relationships.

Dreams that enable us to achieve greater self-understanding, so that deeper, more meaningful relationships are possible.

Sometimes just becoming aware of the deeper parts of ourselves can enable us to build more meaningful relationships with others. One Edgar Cayce reading describes an interesting example of a dream that offered increased self-awareness. This reading was given for a young woman, recently married, who dreamed that she was crying bitterly because her husband wasn't coming home any more. In explaining this dream, Edgar Cayce suggested that the woman's growing love for her husband was awakening an awareness of the pain that separation from him could cause. Though on the surface it seemed distressing, the dream was actually pointing out a very positive potential in this deepening relationship:

> The lesson, then: That of the awakening of the greater relations and forces [that] are coming to exist between the two individuals. Then keep and preserve those in the manner that will bring the better for each. (136-9)

Some dreams help increase our self-understanding by showing us patterns in ourselves that we might want to work on changing. Many dreams have been helpful to me in this respect. In one, I dreamed that I was standing on our porch opening the morning paper, and my wife came downstairs. She poured a cup of coffee and walked onto the porch. I was frustrated at having my time alone disturbed. I thought about going outside and doing the morning chores but decided not to.

Leslie was wearing a light blue dress that she sometimes wore to work, and I made fun of it. I did it very carefully so that my comments were a little ambiguous, but I knew I was making fun of the dress. I tried to laugh about it, but Leslie also knew what I was doing. She became irritated and went out of the house into the driveway. She got into her car, and I knew she was going to work, even though it was very early in the morning.

In the next part of the dream, I was driving Leslie's car down the driveway. She was sitting in the back seat, wearing her blue dress. I felt that I was driving her to work. I woke up embarrassed and frustrated.

As I thought over this dream, I felt that it reflected aspects of a real-life situation in our relationship. The teasing comments I sometimes made about Leslie's work clothes perhaps indicated some uneasiness about her employment. This uneasiness had to do with her becoming more independent. Part of me is fearful of that independence, even though another part of me is proud of it in her work. The dream identified and clarified a pattern of mine in teasing my wife and sometimes hurting her, my motive being an underlying fear of her increasing independence, represented by her work clothes. There may also have been a pun in the dream: I was "driving her to work."

Another dream is a fairly literal reflection of a situation that sometimes occurs, one that I hope is now taking place less frequently. In the dream, we are having dinner at our house with a group of people. Leslie tells a story about me that is funny but somewhat embarrassing. I begin to feel hurt and angry at her for telling the story. As my hurt and anger build in me, I am frustrated that she doesn't sense it.

The scene changes, and I am upstairs hiding in a closet, waiting for Leslie to come up. I still feel remnants of the anger, hurt, and embarrassment as I hear her coming up the stairs. I know that she is still unaware that her story has angered me, but I can't remember what the story was or why the situation has arisen. I am aware that I have blown a tiny event way out of proportion.

In working with this dream, I recalled a number of real-life instances of this kind. It was clear that the dream showed me at least two things to work on. One is a tendency to let minor unintentional hurts become magnified. In the dream I watched this happen and felt it happen inside myself. I was aware that I did not take the opportunity to nip it in the bud. The feeling in the dream was—and my feeling in real life is—that if I don't deal with these minor hurts at once, my sense of pain will grow of its own accord.

The second pattern of behavior has to do with "hiding in the closet"—not letting Leslie know that I have been hurt. This tendency to withdraw and sulk rather than talk things out can be replaced by healthier ways of coping with minor slights. By pointing out these two patterns to me, this dream indicated two ways in which I can build toward deeper and more meaningful relationships.

Dreams that point out opportunities for creative service with others and provide a stimulus toward using those opportunities.

Some years ago I met a psychologist colleague with whom I developed a friendship and working relationship. Within a year of developing that relationship I had a short, vivid dream of being somewhat lost in a huge forest. The forest was beautiful, with fig trees, and had lots of paths that seemed generally familiar to me; nevertheless, as I walked down one of these paths I felt lost and uneasy, but not in any physical pain. I came to a small clearing, and my new friend jumped out of the forest into the clearing. He was dressed like an Indian medicine man or perhaps an African witch doctor. He was wearing a loincloth, his body was painted, and he had feathers and rattles. I was startled, but happy to see him. At this point I realized that I was dressed in a similar way.

As he danced around me, I began to understand that I

was pregnant, although I was a man. In the dream this seemed to be an unusual situation, but not an impossible one. I began to give birth. The process went on for some time, and my friend helped me deliver the baby. Somehow there was no problem with the physical impossibilities. I simply had the baby. Once the birthing started, I was frightened, and I knew that I didn't have complete control. I think not having that control was the most frightening part. As the baby was delivered, I felt a tremendous sense of relief and exhilaration. In the dream, I received a taste of what mothers must experience in real life.

The overall feeling of the dream was that I had been helped by this friend in a deep way that I didn't really understand. Having the baby seemed to represent giving birth to a new part of myself. Thus the dream showed me a potential for creativity and indicated that it could be shared with my friend.

Another dream involved an old friend who was living in another state and whom I hadn't spoken with in a number of years. In the dream I had a telephone call from this man, but I didn't hear his voice on the phone. The operator simply said, "This is a call from Joe Williams. He is sick and needs your help." That was the entire dream.

Although I remembered the dream and wrote it down the next morning, I procrastinated about calling my friend. A few days later I received a call from him and he was, indeed, seriously ill and needed my help. The dream had identified an opportunity for me to offer service within a relationship.

Edgar Cayce gave quite a few readings about dreams in which people were shown how they could help and support the work of others. For example, one woman who devoted a large part of her life to assisting her husband in his work had several encouraging dreams that affirmed the importance of her efforts and indicated ways in which she could be of greatest aid. In one such dream she saw herself correcting a mistake her husband was making. The woman's dream reading assured her that her help was indeed necessary if her husband's activities were to have their best possible results. When she asked how she could assist him most effectively, she was told: " . . . in counsel and advice— for, as has been given, the abilities of the body, of the conscious mind towards things of this nature are far-seeing by the body. Counsel and advice is well from this body." (538-24)

Dreams that present memories of possible past-life experiences.

A number of people were told in their Cayce readings that through their dreams they had the ability to recall past-life experiences. Such readings generally went on to say that there was a reason for these memories, a way in which they could be used constructively in the dreamer's current life. Frequently this purpose involved enabling the dreamer to build more fulfilling relationships with people who had been known in the distant past and were being re-encountered in the present.

In one reading of this type, a woman asked the meaning of a dream she had had about one of her acquaintances. In reply, Cayce stated that the two women had been closely associated with each other during previous incarnations in Egypt and in Atlantis. The dreamer was then told that by searching within herself she would be able to discover much about her former associations with the other woman and that these memories could prove very helpful to both of them in the present:

> . . . as these are delved into, *much* may be gained that will be helpful to each in comprehending that visioned by self, as to how their relations and their associations might aid one another. The vision, then, was

rather an experience where *practical* application may
be made . . . (540-1)

I have experienced several possible past-life scenarios in
dreams that have proved helpful in present relationships. I
once dreamed that I was the father of my present younger
brother. In the dream, he was interested in electronics and
technical things that I didn't grasp and which frightened me.
Rather than trying to understand him and his interests, I
avoided developing a deeper relationship with him and he
ran away. When I heard from his mother that he had run off,
I felt panicky and out of control. I think that this dream and
similar ones reflect a pattern that I face in this life of feeling
the need to control my younger brother. He understand-
ably resists this control. The dreams offered me a chance to
see more clearly my characteristic manner of relating to
him.

One vivid dream of mine portrayed the clothes and scen-
ery of what was perhaps a Mediterranean country in earlier
times. I knew myself in the dream, although my physical
features and clothes were different from the ones I have in
waking life. In the dream I was preparing to deliver a talk or
presentation to a gathering of hundreds of people. I was
very tired and frustrated, and I felt overworked and ill-pre-
pared for my responsibilities involving this project.

While I was feeling this way, several people that I didn't
know approached me. As someone introduced them to me,
I dropped the hand of the first person to take the hand of
the second and looked into their eyes and felt a sense of
trust, reassurance, and help.

In the dream I knew that I had seen that same look and
felt those same feelings when meeting someone I had recently become acquainted with in my present life. This individual was a man in the dream, though in this life she is a
woman. In both the dream and my waking life the person

had similarly distinctive physical characteristics.

When I awakened, I sensed that the two people were the same. The dream has been helpful in encouraging me to look for and draw out that group of very positive, beneficial feelings; and it has helped me realize the value of a particular relationship in which those feelings can be found.

Dreams that provide better understanding of problems being worked on by others with whom we have relationships.
In a dream I am in my backyard at night. In one corner of the yard there's a campfire, and I am curious who the people around the campfire are. I approach the fire, and as I get closer I can hear the people around it carrying on an argument. I recognize two of the main people involved in the disagreement as colleagues at work, and they're arguing about a work situation that also includes me. I feel that I should probably go up to the campfire meeting and discuss the situation, but I don't really want to. So I stay back in the shadows, feeling hidden there.

The scene changes, and I realize that there is a large group of people watching this whole thing; even though it seems to be dark, this is part of a play and I'm really not hidden the way I thought I was. It's as if the corner of the yard is a stage and the stage setting includes what looks like darkness, but I'm not actually hidden at all. I am surprised and frustrated by this, but also sort of happy for some reason.

I think this dream reflects different aspects of my work environment and the people with whom I have relationships there. It helped me understand my attitude of finding it distasteful to get involved in arguments and wanting to avoid conflict. Often this kind of avoidance is superficial; as this dream indicates, it is not always the most constructive way of relating to people in these situations.

Another dream that offered the dreamer a perspective of

a problem faced by someone close to him was described to me by a man concerned about his lack of energy and interest in the sexual aspect of his relationship with his wife. He said that his wife had some of the same feelings.

The dream showed what the man felt might be a past-life situation, in which he was the father of his present wife. In the dream he had sexual feelings toward his daughter, but he did not pursue them. His daughter was aware of these feelings and frightened by them, and in the dream this became a point of difficulty in their relationship. It's possible that this dream enabled the man to see the problem more clearly from his wife's point of view.

Several Cayce readings were given on dreams that helped the dreamers to understand the difficulties of people close to them. In one example, a man dreamed that his wife was working hard to swim through a large body of water, trying to reach someone standing on a high cliff on the opposite shore. The man realized that in order for his wife to reach her goal, she would have to overcome great difficulties, and he became afraid for her. Finally she reached the man on the cliff and handed him a silver cup. At that point, the dreamer realized that the man was himself, and he felt very happy. According to the reading, this dream was a representation of the trouble the woman would have to go through to gain knowledge. The dream's hopeful ending showed the dreamer the possibility of his being able to help his wife and thus to make the relationship more fulfilling:

> The recognition of the work, the hardships, encountered to attain [knowledge] is felt in the inner self of the entity [the dreamer], yet, as is seen through the reaching of the goal, the entity, as has been given, is able to assist and to crown the efforts with success . . . that brings happiness, joy and peace . . . (900-109)

Dreams that give us an opportunity to prepare for approaching conditions that may prove difficult in a relationship.

Some people might expect that it would be quite rare for us to receive this type of aid in our dreams. The ability to obtain advance knowledge of future situations is something many associate only with specially gifted psychics. The Edgar Cayce readings, however, present a very different view of our natural human potential. According to this source, the minds of all of us are in contact at the subconscious level, and the divine spirit within each one of us at times communicates with our conscious minds. Thus we have two means of receiving glimpses of conditions that may be approaching. During sleep we are open to communication via both these avenues.

Quite a few Cayce readings identify individual dreams as presentations of possible developments in the dreamers' lives and associations with others; in fact, one general discourse on the nature of sleep and dreaming plainly states that "There are *no* individuals who haven't at *some time* been warned as respecting that [which] may arise in their daily or physical experience!" (5754-3)

One clear example of such a warning came in a reading for a young woman who dreamed that she, her husband, her mother, and some of her mother's friends were preparing to leave their old home and go to a summer residence. There was a disagreement over where exactly they should go, with several of the friends expressing different opinions. The dreamer's mother became very angry and irritable with her. Edgar Cayce said that this dream was an actual representation of something that could arise in the dreamer's relationship with her mother and the others. His response also suggests that such information is given not to satisfy idle curiosity, but to enable the dreamer to prepare to meet the approaching situation constructively.

This is the presentation . . . of conditions that may be expected, through the relation of the mother and of friends in the old home, becoming irritated and worried at some condition, attitude or position, that will be assumed by this entity. Being forewarned, be prepared. (136-16)

A number of dreams have given me this type of aid in relating to people I work with. Often, when I've been thinking about an upcoming business meeting, I will dream about attitudes of other participants in the meeting ahead of time. I might, for instance, see someone losing his or her temper or someone speaking strongly in favor of a particular issue. This information has frequently proved to be correct and helpful. As another example, I had a series of dreams in which my mother-in-law asked me to go with her on various excursions—to the zoo, to a museum, to the beach, or to play golf—and she always asked me to go with her alone. My feeling in the dreams was one of resistance, of not wanting to be with her, particularly not so frequently nor in situations where we would be alone for long periods of time.

These dreams helped me understand my mother-in-law's interest in establishing a deeper relationship with me and my reluctance to do so. The dreams didn't provide a solution, but they repeatedly called my attention to the need to address the issue. The individual dreams in the series provided different perspectives on the same facet of our association. Like Carl Jung, the Edgar Cayce readings suggest that we could derive great benefit from the study of our serial dreams. This approach seems particularly suitable in regard to relationships, which are frequently the subject of a series of dreams.

Many of the dreams described in the preceding examples illustrate what for me is another important point about using dreams to understand and build relationships. This is the appropriateness of a broad attitude toward dreams that views at least some of them as ongoing commentaries and reflections on relationships. This is quite distinct from approaching a dream with the hope and expectation of finding a single, correct interpretation of it.

For example, it would be possible to interpret my dream about my having a baby with my friend's help as meaning that he is going to help me with a project or perhaps that he has already helped me with one. If this approach is adopted, once the project is completed, the helpfulness of the dream is also at an end. I find it much more valuable to see the dream as providing a reflection of a continual potential within the relationship.

The key is an attitude of willingness to continue working with certain dreams over a period of months or perhaps years. This is especially important with those dreams that feel particularly meaningful or involve significant ongoing aspects of our lives, such as relationships. Continuing to work with a dream—like the sustained study of an extremely rich and deep book, thought system, or musical composition—can yield additional insights as time goes by. This type of dream study is likely to provide greater understanding than can be obtained from looking for the quick answer or interpretation to a dream and then leaving it forgotten in the back pages of one's dream notebook.

For me a key to using some of my dreams as ongoing commentaries on my life has involved simply identifying key people (e.g., my mother-in-law) and settings (e.g., work) and to periodically look back at these dreams as a kind of sequence of ongoing reflections.

13

Activities for Strengthening Love Relationships

Strong love relationships require work and commitment and sharpening our skills in human relations. To help in strengthening or healing relationships—and picking up on the readings' emphasis on application—we have designed a series of exercises. Each of the principles used in the four-teen exercises that follow is based on the Edgar Cayce material, and most of them have been described in the preceding chapters of this book. With each project we've included quotations from the Cayce readings that address the concept being considered.

These exercises are most applicable to a man/woman

relationship. They are likely to prove most beneficial if the two partners engage in them together, but a number of them can also be of value to individuals working alone. Typically, each project is meant to be used over a period of several weeks, though the time needed will vary from one exercise to the next.

A key is to use these projects to move beyond the thinking and talking stages to the actual application of the principles. Depending on the exercise you're working with, this may involve sitting quietly together in meditation and prayer, answering questions with paper and pencil, or doing something together outside the usual setting of your relationship.

Project 1: Shared Personal Stories

One reading answered a familiar question—"If they marry, will they be happy and compatible?"—in this way:

> This, to be sure, is a state that is *made* so; not a thing that exists. For life is living, and its changes that come must be met by each under such circumstances and conditions as to *make* the union . . . more and more worthwhile . . . they each should express themselves as a complement to the best that is in each. (939-1)

The idea of this first project is for two people to share with each other the key aspects of their lives *at this time.* This will give each of them a deeper understanding of the other and allow them to attune to each other more completely. In this way they will become more able to work effectively in concert, enjoy their lives together, and help each other express the best that is within them.

Most of us probably feel that we know the basic elements of the life stories of those with whom we have significant relationships. My experience has been that different parts of our backgrounds and our plans and hopes for the future receive different levels of emphasis and energy at different times in our lives. This exercise should help you focus more clearly on the following question: Where are you now and where is your partner in your life story?

Exercise

During the next month, carve out an hour-and-a-half for each partner to tell his or her personal story. The two stories don't have to be told during a single three-hour session. While each one is being related, it is appropriate for the listener to ask questions to help explain parts that are a bit unclear. Follow each story with fifteen minutes of prayer and meditation together.

You can use the following questions to help prepare your story. Be sure to cover each of these points, but don't limit yourself to them; include anything that you feel is important:

What have been the major events in your past? Include any important memories and any experience that you feel was a crossroads in your life.

Who have been the significant people in your life, and why have they been important?

What talents and weaknesses have you discovered in yourself? When and how did you make these discoveries?

What are the most important current issues in your life? How are they affecting your relationship?

What are your hopes and plans for your future in life? How do you envision the future of your relationship?

This project has helped us understand and appreciate one another's current aspirations—a key to building or restoring a strong bond. Try it once.

Project 2: Ideals

(Q) *Wherein was I failing her, or failing my own soul and its progress?*
(A) Doth God point out thy failings? The law is perfect. Study to show thyself approved unto an ideal. Have ye an ideal—spiritual, mental, material? Do ye keep the faith as ye profess in thy knowledge? Knowledge without works is sin. (815-7)

While I was in graduate school, I tried to work in a fairly intensive way with what I felt were some of the most important concepts in the Edgar Cayce readings. I wanted to clarify for myself what role these ideas were going to play in my life in the future.

One of the concepts that I wrestled with was ideals. I really struggled to set ideals for myself, writing meaningful words and phrases in three columns, for my physical, mental, and spiritual ideals. I also wanted just to understand more clearly what the word *ideal* meant to me and what were specific examples of ideals.

In the course of that effort I came upon the idea of describing on paper what would be an ideal day for me at some point in the future. I set that point far enough ahead so that my rational, conscious mind wouldn't encompass that period, since my current plans weren't extended that far out in time. For the next six weeks I spent a portion of just about every day fantasizing and writing down what an ideal day in my life seven years in the future would be.

After I had completed this written description, I set it aside for a long while. Seven years later I returned to it and read it through. I was amazed to discover that much of what I had put down as an ideal day seven years earlier was now manifesting in my life.

This little experiment showed me that as we put energy

into clarifying aspects of our lives in this way, we make it possible for deeper levels of the mind to act on what we have set up. If we're clear enough on what direction we want to take, choices are made—even without our realizing it—that move us in that direction.

Little examples of this type happen all the time. They can make us aware that the mind frequently functions on at least two different levels at once. For instance, many of us have this type of experience when we get into the car to drive somewhere. We start thinking about a decision we have to make or a problem that must be solved. Twenty minutes later we find ourselves at the grocery store, our place of work, or wherever our destination might have been. We don't have any conscious recall of making the decisions to turn left, turn right, or stop at the various stop lights; but there we are. Somehow the decisions were made at an automatic level.

I think the same kind of process can take place when we set our ideals. If we're really clear about them and strongly motivated by them, we'll often find that the choices we make are in line with those ideals, even though we might not have consciously thought through our decisions. We just move ourselves toward the ideals we've set.

That was certainly the case with me. At the end of the seven-year period, I didn't have clear recall of having made all the decisions that had moved me toward my ideal; but I found that that was the direction my life had taken.

Personal experiences like this, accounts others have shared with me, and the importance given ideals in the Cayce readings have combined to convince me that it can be extremely helpful to think about what an ideal relationship would be at some point in the future. This is something that a man and a woman can work out together, and it is something for an individual to utilize, as I did in graduate school. As we develop a clear picture of our ideal relationship and as we put energy into clarifying that picture, we can set forces in motion that will move our lives in the direction we've chosen. An important part of this type of work is to return periodically for further clarification of the ideal relationship, because ideals can change with time.

The positive effects that a couple can experience through setting and striving toward a shared ideal were described by Cayce as follows:

> If the ideals, if the desires as to the purpose of activity in the material world are in accord, these then will bring harmonious material experiences . . . [and the couple] may be very sure that the outcome of their oneness of purpose will bring a strength that will build constructive experiences . . . (1173-9)

Exercise

This project is designed to help you clarify your ideals with regard to your love relationships. The Edgar Cayce material repeatedly emphasizes the importance of identifying our ideals clearly. As one person was told, " . . . the most important experience of this or any individual entity is to first know what *is* the ideal—spiritually." (357-13) The readings suggest that achieving this knowledge is a lifelong project. Nevertheless, a short-term exercise like ours can be a valuable starting point for the longer-range identification and clarification of ideals.

Start by sitting down alone or with your partner and simply talking (thinking) over your lives together, as in Project 1. Decide what some of the most important parts of your relationship are. Many people list such subjects as children, work, other family members, and friends. Perhaps the chapter headings of this book will suggest suitable topics on which you and your partner can focus. Once you have decided on the major aspects of your relationship, just think out loud, discussing what your ideals would be with regard to each of these subjects.

Consider your ideals on the spiritual, mental, and physical levels. Your spiritual ideal for your relationship is the essential quality you want to guide your lives together. Your mental and physical ideals are the attitudes and actions that will move you in the direction you want to go. It's important that you be specific in these two areas, for it is by taking concrete measures that you will be able to bring your spiritual ideal into manifestation in daily life.

Once you've had a chance to talk over your ideals, use a pencil and paper to develop a picture of your *relationship as it is now.* Divide the paper into three columns and label them "physical," "mental," and "spiritual." (See p. 175 for our sample.) In the left margin, list several areas of your relationship to which you currently devote significant amounts of time and energy. In each column, enter words and phrases that describe those aspects of your lives together. Actions, places, and items would go in the "physical" column; attitudes, emotions, and mental activities would be entered in the "mental" column; and the word or phrase that you feel represents the essential quality of that aspect of your lives together would go in the "spiritual" column. Don't worry too much about getting everything in the right place. The main thing here is to paint an actual picture of these areas of your relationship as it currently exists.

Next, on a separate sheet of paper, describe certain aspects of *your ideal relationship.* Once again divide the sheet into three columns, labeled "physical," "mental," and "spiritual." (See p. 176.) Then divide the paper into three horizontal sections. Check the first chart you completed in this exercise, and choose three of the areas of your relationship on which you are spending significant amounts of time and energy. Write these subjects in the left margin of each of the three sections.

Now choose a word or phrase that represents your spiritual ideal with regard to your relationship as a whole. One technique that can help you come up with a suitable expression is to spend a little time remembering experiences with your partner that were most deeply spiritual and meaningful to you. For your spiritual ideal you might want to select a word or phrase (for example, "loving equals") that elicits the feelings of those memories. Enter this expression in the right-hand column. Since this is the quality you wish to build in your entire relationship, it will be the same for all the three areas of life on which you've chosen to focus.

The next step is to identify your mental and physical ideals for each of these three aspects of your relationship. For each of these areas, list in the column labeled "mental" some attitudes you could hold that might move your relationship closer to the spiritual ideal you've selected. There will probably be several suitable attitudes to be entered for each person and each aspect of the relationship. Now for each area you're working on, think of actions and behaviors that would move the relationship closer to your mental and spiritual ideals. List these actions in the appropriate section of the column for your physical ideals.

After you've completed the two charts, take a close look at the differences between the chart that shows your relationship as it actually is now and the one that represents your ideal relationship. During the next three weeks, spend one hour each week discussing the two charts with each other. You might find that modifying some of the entries you've made or adding new items to your lists will give your ideals added clarity. Also discuss and try to take some steps mentally and physically that would help move your relationship toward your spiritual ideal.

Project 3: Pray and Meditate Together

... when doubts and fears and troubles arise ...
come ye rather together before the Throne of grace

The Relationship Now

	Physical	Mental	Spiritual
Children			
Finances			
The Farm			
Our Jobs			
Sex and Intimacy			
Our Close Friends			

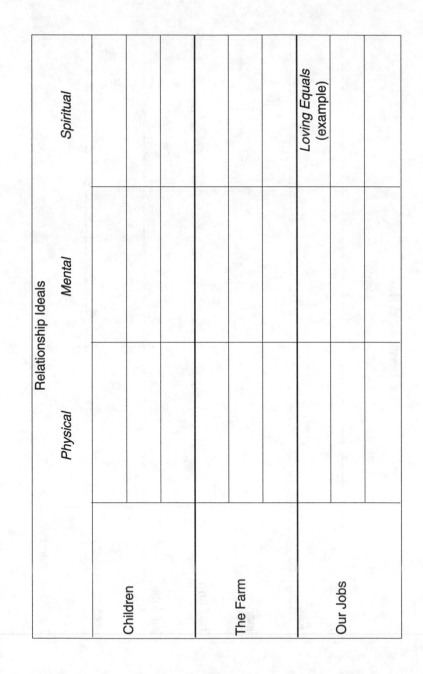

	Relationship Ideals		
	Physical	*Mental*	*Spiritual*
Children			
The Farm			
Our Jobs			*Loving Equals* (example)

and mercy, as may be found in the meditation before the Lord. Take thine troubles to Him, not to thy fellow man! For *He* is merciful when *man* may be unkind ..."(480-20)

The Edgar Cayce material's guidance regarding attunement centers on prayer and meditation. Though these two practices are closely related to each other, they are not the same. One statement of the difference between them is that in prayer we speak to God, while in meditation we still the body and the conscious mind and listen for God to communicate with us. The basic principle behind meditation is that the spirit of God with which we were endowed at our creation remains within us forever. It will manifest itself to us if we turn our attention away from the self-oriented parts of our lives and focus on it. By doing so, we can develop our awareness of God's will for us, and we can receive guidance in following His will in all that we do. (*Reflections on the Path* by H.B. Puryear is an excellent further reference on meditation.)

There are several ways in which practicing meditation and prayer with someone with whom we're building a relationship can be a healthy addition to people to recognize that there are deeper energies, forces, and levels of consciousness at work than the ones that appear to fuel so much of our activity and conversation on the surface. Once these more profound, spiritual aspects of our nature have been acknowledged, the commitment of this regular time together can enable us to achieve balance and healing at these deeper levels. Meditation opens up the possibility of balancing our deeper energies; and prayer, in my opinion, provides a very real opportunity for us to channel these healing energies toward our partner in the relationship. The aid and comfort that can be found in joint prayer and meditation are clearly described in several Cayce readings, such as the following:

Then when ye are, either of thee, in turmoil—*not*
one shall do *all* the praying, nor all the "cussing"; but
together—ask! and He will give—as He has promised—
that assurance of peace, of harmony, that can *only* come
from a coordinated, cooperative effort . . . (1523-6)

In meditation, according to the Cayce material, we step
back from the structures and patterns of the conscious
mind and listen to our higher self, our spiritual nature. As
one reading expresses it, "Let earth, and earthly things keep
silent. Then ye may hear the way of truth." (3376-2) By
meditating with another person, we practice together this
stepping back and listening. We share with each other our
endeavor to reach the deeper energies within us, and in so
doing we magnify the potential of these energies to influence our relationship.

Balancing our deeper energies is related to the age-old
concept of each person's androgynous nature. In the last
fifty years, perhaps beginning with the work of C.G. Jung,
there has been a refocusing of attention on this idea. Jung
suggested that the male and female aspects of being, which
he called the *animus* and the *anima,* are essential compo-
nents in the makeup of every man and woman. These two
principles—archetypes, in Jungian terms—must be understood and acknowledged as existing within each of us.

The ancient Chinese terms of *yin* and *yang* seem to refer
to the same basic qualities. These principles are sometimes
seen as corresponding to heaven and earth. The earth embodies solidity, groundedness, and receptivity, while
heaven involves openness and light. Yang is often related to
heaven, sky, and bright sunshine, yin to darkness or clouds
and the moist, receptive earth.

Rudolf Steiner, in his lectures on the "Study of Man,"
seems to describe these same two principles or forces working within each of us. He calls them the principles of sym-

pathy and antipathy. Antipathy separates us from the world; it is rational and analytical. Sympathy involves us with the world and with other people.

My sense is that at some deep level meditation helps us balance these two forces. It entails not only a balancing of the energies of the body at the physical and deeper levels, but also a balancing between our involvement with the outer world and our inner selves. A similar type of equilibrium is important in many sports, such as skiing and surfing, in which a balance between tenseness and relaxation must be maintained. The same sense of balance is a part of the meditation process.

Balance is also necessary in relationships. We need, as always, a certain amount of independence; and yet at the same time we feel the need for the connectedness that comes in a relationship. There is the pressure to diffuse our individual boundaries with those of the other person. But if those boundaries become too diffuse, problems usually arise.

The hoped-for equilibrium between maintaining one's individuality in a relationship and merging with one's partner closely parallels the balance sought in meditation, which involves being in the earth and yet somehow letting go. I feel that in furnishing an opportunity for two people to practice attaining this balance together, shared meditation can play a very important, helpful role in one's inner life and in a relationship.

Exercise

In my counseling of people involved in difficult relationships, no suggestion has proved more helpful than prayer and meditation together—and none has been resisted more vigorously. Try it with your partner, five days a week for a month.

- Read or reread a good book on prayer and meditation.

- Choose a twenty-minute period each day that is convenient for both of you. It's not absolutely necessary for you to be in the same location, but do meditate at the same time as the other. You can adjust the time if you have to, though you'll probably find that the project goes more smoothly if you try to stay with the same time for most of the month.
- Spend fifteen minutes each day in the silence of meditation. Then, for five minutes, pray for each other and for your relationship. If you are physically present with each other, try praying out loud.
- As you progress through the month, check off the days you pray and meditate together on a chart like the one below. Putting the sheet where you can see it each day can help you maintain your motivation. Persistence and patience are very important to this exercise; as Edgar Cayce told one spiritual seeker, "ye must learn to meditate, just as ye have learned to walk, to talk, to do any of the physical attributes of thy mind . . . " (281-41)

	Week 1	Week 2	Week 3	Week 4
Sunday				
Monday				
Tuesday				
Wednesday				
Thursday				
Friday				
Saturday				

Project 4: Shared Dreams

Man approaches the nearer condition of its approach to [God] when the normal is at rest; sleep or slumber . . . it is the individual's job . . . to understand if they will study, to show themselves approved . . . In this age, at present, 1923, there is not sufficient credence given dreams; for the best development of the human family is to give the greater increase in knowledge of the subconscious, soul or spirit world. This is a dream. (3744-5)

Self-understanding is of great importance to anyone seeking to fulfill his or her highest potential in life. To make the best use of our strengths and avoid the pitfalls brought about by our weaknesses, we must know where those strengths and weaknesses lie. And, as the above passage indicates, we must strive not only to know ourselves as individuals, but to understand how we function in relation to others. The subconscious mind can be a valuable source of assistance in this effort. In our dreams it can present us with information beyond that which is ordinarily available to the conscious mind: " . . . dreams are that of which the subconscious is made, for any [personal] conditions ever becoming reality is first dreamed." (136-7) But today, just as in 1923, many of us don't pay sufficient attention to our dreams. Thus we close ourselves off to the self-understanding they would provide.

For most of us, consistent effort is needed in order to derive the full benefit from our dreams. It takes practice to remember and interpret correctly these messages from the deeper aspects of ourselves. As we put forth this effort, we demonstrate to the subconscious that we're seriously interested in hearing what it has to say. This in itself often stimulates an increase in the number and clarity of dreams we receive.

Exercise

The purpose of this exercise is to encourage you to pay closer attention to your dreams, particularly ones that might furnish greater insight into your relationship. For the coming month, do the following:

• Read or review a good book on understanding your dreams.

• Commit yourself to spending one-half hour three times a week with your partner discussing your dreams, especially those that seem to deal with your relationship.

A. Put a notebook for recording your dreams by your bed. Record your dreams as soon as possible after awakening.

B. Each night as you fall asleep, suggest to yourself, "I am especially interested in dreams that will help in my relationship with _____. I will remember my dreams."

C. Look for these elements in your dreams: people; setting; action; feelings; words; and specific objects, animals, and symbols.

D. If a loved one appears in a dream, assume that the dream is about your association. For every dream you record during the month, start with the hypothesis that it concerns your relationships. This might not actually be the case, and for some dreams you may have to move on to other possible interpretations. But the deeper parts of the mind can respond to the suggestion to focus dreams on a specific aspect of life. If you consistently show an interest in your relationship, you may well find that a surprising number of dreams will provide insight into this area.

It is important to remember that dreams often simply reflect areas of imbalance or stress and don't always provide a solution. But at the very least dreams can provide a focus for discussing some of these difficult areas of the relationship and thus start a process of clarifying and healing. Also, on occasion, you will be amazed at the helpful insight provided by a dream discussed together. I can almost guarantee it!

Project 5: Clarifying Priorities, Simplifying Our Lives

... if there are put the first things first and the proper evaluations of those of material and mental and spiritual forces, then there may be a life of harmony, a life of happiness, a life of joy in this experience. For it will make all of those whom the entity may contact day by day aware . . . that he hath taken thought of his relationships to his God and his fellow man! (1349-1)

I feel that a regular focus on simplifying our lives is one of our most important tools for building healthier relationships. We can make our lives less complex in general, and we can concentrate specifically on simplifying the areas that involve another person. Both steps are likely to benefit our relationship. The basic idea is to decide what is truly important and then to de-emphasize the things that are comparatively insignificant. This will allow us to devote more of ourselves to building the parts that really do matter.

In working on our relationship, Leslie and I can simplify our lives together. These talks provide an opportunity for us to clarify our priorities, and they have been a valuable part of our effort to identify our ideals.

One factor that often has an important effect on the success of a project is the degree to which we can put aside distractions and devote meaningful amounts of our energy and attention to whatever we are trying to accomplish. This is true of our business projects, our efforts at self-improvement, and our creative, artistic endeavors. It is also true, to some degree, of our relationships.

But many of us find it hard to focus on our relationships as much as we would like. It seems that in our current society the "natural flow of things" somehow causes our lives to become more complex—more filled with activities and distractions that are not related to our true purposes. In today's world it can require active effort to keep our priorities clear and our lives simple.

I often find that my own life is being complicated by concerns that I wouldn't consider high-priority items, but which nevertheless seem to require large amounts of time, energy, and attention. For example, I buy new gadgets, tools, and kitchen appliances for their "added convenience" and to save time; then I often spend significant chunks of time and energy figuring them out, fixing them, or just keeping track of them. My IRA gets larger, and I find myself spending time and energy on the details of investing, rather than taking one of several responsible steps that would simplify this area of my life. I spend time worrying about and resisting Leslie's close friendships, rather than accepting them and thus eliminating what is for me a needless energy drain. These days it seems that every time we blink we can find our lives more cluttered with things that distract us from our focus on building healthy, happy relationships.

Exercise

This exercise is designed to help you define more clearly exactly which areas of your life and your relationship are most important. This will help you identify some that could be simplified or perhaps even eliminated on a trial basis. You will then be able to devote more of your energy and attention to the things that matter most to you.

The chart opposite provides an opportunity for you and, if possible, your partner to list five high-priority aspects of your life. Then it asks you to list five items that you feel are comparatively unimportant, but that seem to take an inordinate amount of your attention and energy.

Your entries in the second list will be parts of your life

that you might feel need to be simplified. This can sometimes be achieved through clarification. Some aspects of our lives can seem complex only because they are unclear to us, and we spend a certain amount of our attention worrying about them because of their lack of clarity.

After you have completed the second list, discuss with your partner what measures you can take to simplify these areas of your life.

Simplifying Our Lives

List five high-priority aspects of your life now.

1. _____

2. _____

3. _____

4. _____

5. _____

List five aspects of your life that you consider low priority, but which seem to take unwarranted amounts of time and attention. Remember that just worrying about something is one way of spending time and energy on it.

1. _____

2. _____

3. _____

4. _____

5. _____

Project 6: Forgiveness

When anger hath beset thee, hast thou stopped and considered what the fruit of rash words would bring? . . .

How hath it been given? If ye would be forgiven, ye must forgive. If ye would know love, ye must be lovely. If ye would have *life, give* it! What is life? *God!*—in action with thy fellow man! (793-2)

Years ago we were talking about forgiveness in our Search for God study group.* We commiserated over the difficulty we can have in letting go of the anger we sometimes feel toward those with whom we have the closest relationships. We agreed that though in many cases there is an opportunity to release and forgive, we often choose to hold onto the hurt or the resentment a little longer. Perhaps we feel that by keeping our anger and our pain alive we are somehow getting even with the person who caused them. In most cases this feeling is mistaken, but it's one by which a lot of us seem to be affected.

The next week, one of the members of our group brought in a newspaper story that he felt illustrated our frequent predicament. I'm not certain how true it is, but each time I tell this story I can identify with the characters in it very easily. I know it touches a point of reality and sensitivity in me.

The incident involved a husband and a wife who got into an argument while they were having breakfast together. They differed on the subject being discussed, and each became more and more frustrated and angry at the other's

---

*The A.R.E. sponsors hundreds of Search for God study groups throughout the world. These small, informal groups meet, typically on a weekly basis, to talk about the basic ideas on spiritual growth presented in the Edgar Cayce readings and related materials. Such groups provide an excellent opportunity for members to discuss and apply the kind of ideas that are described in this book.

unwillingness to be persuaded. Each of them became more firmly entrenched in his or her own position and increasingly irritated with the other person.

It reached the time for the wife, a schoolteacher, to go to work. She went upstairs and put on her favorite dress, which had to be zipped all the way up the back. She then returned to the kitchen and asked her husband to zip her up. This was probably the opportunity for them both to forgive and release the situation. The husband could have zipped up the dress and given his wife a hug. They could have told each other they really did love each other, and the argument would have been over.

The husband, however, could not bring himself to do this. He was still sitting in the kitchen, growing more and more irritated over their disagreement. When his wife asked him to zip up her dress, he vented some of his anger and frustration by yanking the zipper up and down and up and down as hard as he could. The zipper ripped out of the dress—his wife's favorite one. Now she was really angry. She stomped upstairs, changed clothes, and went off to school. She spent the day thinking of how she could get even. (I can imagine some of us doing this over entire lifetimes!)

When school was over and the woman came home, she was surprised to find her husband's car in the driveway, since he usually arrived home after she did. As she walked up the front walk she saw what she assumed was her husband under the car working on the engine. He was on his back with his legs sticking out from under the front of the car. The woman smiled to herself as she saw her opportunity to get even. She marched over to him, took hold of the zipper on his pants, and lifted him off the ground as she yanked it back and forth and back and forth with all her might. He twisted and jumped under the car and then lay still.

She marched into the house with a feeling of satisfaction over having gotten even. To her horror, there in the kitchen was her husband, seated at the table with the afternoon newspaper. "Who is that out under the car?" she screamed. Puzzled over her excitement, he said that it was their neighbor, who had come over to work on the car that afternoon. The wife described what she had done, and they ran out to the car together.

The neighbor was still under the front of the car. They pulled him out and found that he was unconscious, with a gash on his forehead. When they revived him, he said that when he felt the zipper on his pants beginning to move, it had startled him so much that he must have had a giant reflex reaction, hit his head under the car, and knocked himself out.

This story clearly shows how we can get caught if we hold onto our feelings of anger and try to get even with those who have caused us pain and frustration. I think many of us can identify with the husband as he neglects the opportunity to release and forgive and angrily yanks his wife's zipper up and down. And many of us would fall into the same trap as the wife, who holds onto her own anger and tries to get even, only to find it doubling back on her and catching her in the end. This incident illustrates a point made in several Edgar Cayce readings: "Those, then, who hold animosity, hold grudges are building for themselves that which they must meet in confusion, in abuse of self, abuse of others . . ." (2072-15)

I have told this story hundreds of times, and still I can recognize that same pattern of behavior in myself. It crops up from time to time in my relationship with my wife. One situation in which it sometimes becomes evident occurs when we have visitors over for meals. Like many families, at these get-togethers we often share experiences and stories. Sometimes Leslie will tell a story or do some other little thing that hurts my feelings for some reason. At times my response is to feel sorry for myself, to withdraw at least a little bit, and to pout.

We have a kind of unspoken agreement that we won't try to sort out this type of issue while the guests are there, and so the conversation continues. Typically, the meal ends, the visitors leave, and we complete the day's activities without Leslie even knowing that I've been hurt or that there is anything wrong. The only indication she might have is that I'm a little more withdrawn than usual.

Most nights, after the children are asleep and things are finally quiet and we are in bed together, we simply touch feet to acknowledge that we're both there and to reconnect. But not on those days when she has hurt my feelings! I lie on my side of the bed like a mummy, pretending that there is nothing wrong, but careful not to have my feet touch hers. I find myself holding onto my hurt and frustration and feeling that somehow I am getting even with her by holding back in this way—even though she might not even know that there is a specific problem.

Leslie does a good job of helping me learn to talk about such hurts, that in the talking there can come better understanding, release, and forgiveness. Sometimes she does this with gentle teasing or joking about my withdrawal after the situation has passed. Mainly, I think I have learned through watching her example of speaking up and the positive results that usually follow. With her help, I think I've become a little better at handling this type of situation.

Over many years I watched my father counsel individuals who were having problems with their relationships. Often these problems involved one partner's inability to forgive the other. Dad would share his understanding of his father's readings on the subject and the insight he had gathered in his own experiences with relationships.

He developed a simple exercise to help people overcome their reluctance to let go of their pain and their desire to get even. This exercise takes just fifteen or twenty minutes per day; but when used persistently by someone really wanting to heal a relationship, it can be the catalyst for lasting change. Try using it daily during any period of difficulty you experience in a relationship.

Exercise

Read each of the following six questions to yourself and spend several minutes thinking about and writing each response. Then take some time to pray for your relationship, yourself, and your loved one. Offer each of the prayers of forgiveness described at the end of the questions.

1. When did you first love this person? Answer not with dates, but with experiences that produced your feelings of love.

2. What was an early difficulty you had with this individual? What was the basic cause of this difficulty?

3. What is the most irritating thing about this person?

4. Have you ever feared this person? What was the occasion?

5. Have you ever wanted to hurt this person? Strike this person? Kill this person?

6. Have you ever felt any relationship with this person other than that which now exists (for example, as a father, mother, brother, sister, loved one, or friend)?

A. We know that God has already forgiven us, so pray that you may accept this forgiveness wherever it is needed in your relationship.
B. Pray to forgive yourself for specific things you have done in this relationship.
C. Pray to forgive the other person for any hurt he or she has caused you.
D. Pray for this person. Bless this person. Surround him or her with light.
E. Give thanks to God for your opportunities to experience love.

Project 7: Emphasize the Positive

For it will bring the greater blessings, the greater glories, the greater contentment, the greater satisfaction; the glorious harmony of adjusting thyself and thy relationships one with another in making same ever harmonious . . .

In *every* association. . . let thy activities be . . . *directed* by the spirit of *hopefulness, helpfulness,* in thy attitudes one to another. (480-20)

A great many of the Edgar Cayce readings dealing with

difficult relationships suggested that each person focus on the strengths and positive qualities of the other. The word *magnify* was often used in readings of this sort; for example, one seeker was advised to "Magnify the virtues of all . . . thy attempts to be holy . . ." (3621-l) In the context of a relationship, I take this use of *magnify* to mean that we should pay more attention to our loved one's strong points. One good way of doing this is simply to talk about these characteristics and compliment our loved one on them more frequently.

I certainly don't think it is healthy to sweep the problems in a relationship under the rug, especially what seems to be a recurring pattern, like my tendency to withdraw, for example. In this section, we have suggested several ways of approaching those difficult areas. My experience has been that some troublesome areas need to be discussed; however, giving more attention to our partner's positive attributes on a day-to-day basis with our comments and praise is a more effective way of strengthening the relationship.

The importance of emphasizing the positive was vividly illustrated to me during the course of my work in graduate school. One of my projects there involved doing some consultation with Head Start programs, which engaged a large number of volunteers in trying to help develop pre-school activities. I remember so clearly my experience with a volunteer teacher who had perhaps twenty-five pre-school children in her class. On the wall she had hung a large chart with each child's name in a column down the left, and the days of the week and month listed across the top. Each day the children could get gold stars by their names.

The problem was that the teacher had arranged the system so that the children who misbehaved were the ones who received the gold stars. I think the idea was to embarrass the youngsters who acted up by using the stars to call attention to their misbehavior. Many of the children ended up with long rows of gold stars by their names. In talking with these young people, I found that they seemed very proud of their stars. The teacher had made the mistake of setting up her system backward; she was paying attention to and magnifying undesirable behaviors, rather than rewarding positive ones.

I think our interactions in relationships often work the same way. Many of us have a tendency to complain about what bothers us regarding other people. There is a good deal of research to show that this kind of attention is not a particularly effective tool for building a person's positive attributes. It is much more fruitful to reward and encourage the behaviors and qualities that we feel should be strengthened. This psychological principle is recognized in an admonition found in many Cayce readings: "We would minimize the faults, we would magnify the virtues." (3640-1) As we pay more attention to a person's positive characteristics, these attributes become even stronger, through reinforcement.

The principle of reinforcement is a basic one in psychology. Its validity and strength plus the power of attention as a reward or reinforcement were illustrated for me, early in graduate school, while I was teaching a class in Introductory Psychology. Our topic was the classic studies showing that rats and other animals that were rewarded with food for exhibiting specific behaviors increased the frequency of those behaviors. From there, we began talking about how the same idea can be applied with children and adults.

Without my knowing it, the class decided to test this principle on me. They picked a particular behavior to reinforce—in this case, it was nodding my head—and they chose attention as the reward they would use. Their plan was to ask more questions in class, increase their contributions to our discussions, and, in general, show more attention whenever I would nod my head up and down. They decided to continue this experiment for one month.

The room we were meeting in was also used for observing children at play, and it had a one-way mirror in one of its walls. The class had someone film about half of our first session during the test period, and they measured in seconds the amount of time I spent nodding my head. Throughout the following month they gradually increased their class participation and the number of questions they asked whenever I would nod. At the end of the month they filmed me for another thirty minutes and measured the amount of time I spent exhibiting the chosen behavior.

The results were amazing! During the first period of filming I nodded my head for a total time of less than one minute. At the end of the month, I spent virtually the whole time on film nodding. During the entire month I had no idea that the experiment was being conducted, and I had no conscious awareness of any change in my pattern of behavior.

Now, I'm not suggesting that we manipulate each other in our relationships in this way. But realizing the power of reinforcement can help us choose responses to our loved ones that will build and magnify the positive aspects of our associations.

Exercise

Focusing attention on the positive qualities of a relationship or another person can strengthen those characteristics and increase the frequency with which they are expressed. This, I feel, is what the Cayce readings are referring to when they encourage us to *magnify* the virtues in others. The purpose of this exercise is to help you focus on the positive in your relationship and in your partner. This is something you can work on either by yourself or with your loved one.

Begin by listing the positive qualities in the other person.

You'll be referring to this list throughout the exercise, so it's a good idea to keep it in a notebook or some other place where it will be easy to get to. Write down your partner's strengths and the personal characteristics he or she brings to the relationship that build and heal it. For example, you could list a sense of humor or a willingness to talk about potential problems before they have a chance to affect other aspects of your lives together. You might want to develop your list by spending several periods reflecting on the relationship and your partner. Discussions between the two of you could be included in this stage of the project.

Over the next month, focus your attention on building these strengths in your relationship. At least five times a week, look over the list at the beginning of the day, choose one of the positive attributes from it, and make it a point to magnify this quality throughout the day. This can be done, for example, by talking about this characteristic of your loved one and complimenting him or her on it. You will probably discover other ways in which you can call attention to this feature and show your appreciation for it. Be alert for these opportunities and take full advantage of them when they arise.

You might choose to focus on a different positive characteristic every day. Another possibility is to continue reinforcing the same strength over a longer period, but each day to magnify it in a different way.

At the end of the day, make a note of the aspect of the other person or of your relationship that you have tried to strengthen. If possible, take a few minutes to write out a description of how you paid attention to this quality and what the result was.

When the month is over, look back and note any effects this experiment has had on your overall relationship. Notice any "new" ones? This is another step that can involve discussions with your loved one.

Project 8: Past-Life Patterns in Present Relationships

Individuals do not meet by chance. They *are* necessary in the experiences of others, though they may not always use their opportunities in a spiritual way or manner. (2751-1)

Edgar Cayce was asked many questions by people who were trying to understand their relationships better. His responses to these questions often included descriptions of associations between the individuals in past lives. Here are several examples that illustrate how past-life relationships can influence a couple's current life together:

(Q) How was I associated with my present family in previous incarnations; first, my wife ... ?
(A) As the father of the present wife in the experience before this, and didn't always make it easy for any—owing to associations with others! Also in the Palestine activity ye were closely associated as the companion or husband of the one who is the present wife. Again in Atlantis, the associations were rather as acquaintances and helpful influences one to the other—yet questions oft as to one another. (2301-1)

(Q) How was I associated with my present wife ... in Palestine?
(A) She was then the entity's daughter. Doesn't she try to boss him now? As the associations come ... the entity has chosen well ... we will find much help, mentally, materially, spiritually. (1003-2)

(Q) What was my relationship in the past incarnations with Robert ... ? Explain the present urges from these associations.
(A) In the English experience, very unsatisfactory— because he left thee and ye never quite lost sight of the

manner in which ye were treated. And doubts have arisen. Yet there are those obligations, those things to be worked out together yet ...

(Q) Should my present relationship with him remain closed?

(A) It will be opened of itself, for it is not finished as yet.

(Q) What attitude should I hold for our mutual development?

(A) As ye would be forgiven, forgive. (2791-1)

Sometimes imagining a possible condition from an earlier lifetime can help us understand and deal with a pattern affecting our current associations. Leslie and I have used this technique in working on a kind of father/daughter pattern that we've found appearing in our relationship at times. I am sure that it has been influenced by my being ten years older than Leslie and by her having had to adopt and adjust to a number of conditions that were already existing in my life; for instance, she had to move into the home and community where I was already living. There was a tendency, especially early in our relationship, for me to take more of an initiative in making decisions affecting our lives.

As I thought about this pattern, I could easily imagine a possible past-life situation in which this kind of dependency relationship could have developed to the point where it was not beneficial for either of us. Leslie and I have discussed this possibility, and I feel that doing so has helped me better understand this part of our lives together. I can now see that in the current lifetime we have an opportunity to move through the unhealthy aspects of this kind of control/dependency association.

Another potentially helpful way of looking at patterns in a relationship involves using some of the philosophical premises of Jungian analysis. In an article in a book entitled *Challenge of the Heart,* edited by John Welwood, the Jungian analyst Robert Stein writes about the neglected child within. He suggests that a major problem in modern marriages arises when a neglected inner child within each partner begins to influence the relationship. The energy of this neglected, unfulfilled child demands care and attention and creates complexities and resentment.

The author suggests that the difficulties produced by this child energy come about both because our culture does not provide the necessary social and psychological structures for moving from childhood into adulthood, and because of blocks between each individual adult and his or her own parents. According to Stein, as we work on a relationship—particularly a marriage relationship—it is important for each of us to make the necessary psychic separation from our parents and to understand and move through the pulls and pushes of the inner child.

Exercise

In this exercise, you and your partner will be imagining past-life scenarios that could account for certain patterns in your present relationship.

The first step is for each person to list two recurring themes or patterns in the current relationship that he or she would like to understand better.

Next, each person is to describe on the same page a possible past-life scenario that might have produced each of the current situations listed. (Perhaps start with a dream fragment or a dèjá vu feeling.) Use your imagination and a bit of quiet time to help you come up with the past-life scenarios.

The purpose is to give you a different and perhaps a better understanding of these patterns and their possible causes. This will allow you to replace habitual, automatic reactions to the situations with responses based on a more complete perception of them.

Finally, discuss your imagined past-life patterns together and see if they enable you to view the current condition in a more helpful light.

Project 9: Commitment

This relationship which is the experience of each, must be accepted by each as a responsibility of one for the other, as one to the other . . .
. . . before God and man there was the promise taken "Until death do us part!" This is not idle; these [individuals] were brought together because there are those conditions wherein each can be a complement to the other. Are these to be denied? (2811-3)

In his classic work, *The Art of Loving,* Erich Fromm expresses his uneasiness over our tendency to look for quick, simple answers. In so many of our activities we try to discover easy prescriptions that we can follow.

Our search for an easy-to-follow formula extends to our attempts at the practice of love, which Fromm compares to the practice of Zen. In this area of life, we might talk of the necessary supreme concern as a serious commitment to love and to building a relationship. The author gives the following description of our efforts when this commitment is missing:

If the art is not something of supreme importance, the apprentice will never learn it. He'll remain at best, a good dilettante, but will never become a master. This condition is as necessary for the art of loving as for any other art. It seems, though, as if the proportion between masters and dilettantes is more heavily weighted in favor of the dilettantes in the art of loving than is the case with other arts.

Commitment depends upon a kind of trust and faith in whatever we are committing ourselves to. Fromm distinguishes between irrational and rational faith. The first is an unthinking acceptance of and submission to higher authority; the second, a conviction based on personal experience and thoughtfulness. If we are to develop a deep commitment to a relationship, we must build and maintain within ourselves this second type of faith toward both the structure of our relationship and the person with whom we are associated. When this faith is shaken, we need to work toward reestablishing it.

Serious commitment to anything, including a relationship or another person, is reflected by giving a high priority to it. This concept is expressed in the familiar Bible verse, " . . . where your treasure is, there will your heart be also." (Matthew 6:21) Our use of our time, energy, and money should reflect our commitments. It has been said that if you show a person your cancelled checks, he or she will be able to tell you what is important in your life.

If a relationship is truly important to us, this priority will be reflected in the amount of time, energy, and resources we devote to it. Our commitment will be expressed through such activities as helping the other person progress toward fulfillment, treating him or her with loyalty and truthfulness, and being willing to move past immediate minor issues for the sake of the long-term health of the relationship.

Exercise

The purpose of this project is twofold: first, to help you identify how much time and energy you are committing to a relationship; and second, to encourage you to increase that commitment.

Start by listing the amount of time you spend on various activities during a typical week. Don't just approximate the amount of time you think you spend on each item. Actually keep track of your use of time during an average week. The first chart below will help you with this.

Next, for the same week, list the amount of time you spend with your partner in relationship activities. These entries can overlap or be included in the ones from your first list. The second chart also includes some idea of the types of activities to consider.

Finally, increase the amount of time you commit to the relationship by three hours per week. As part of this increase, spend at least twenty minutes per day, three times a week, talking with your partner about your relationship. The third chart will help you keep track of the time you devote to your relationship during these weeks of increased commitment.

1.   Activity

Hours

Work   _____

Travel   _____

Meals   _____

Sleep   _____

Household chores   _____

TV, video, movies   _____

_____   _____

_____   _____

_____   _____

_____   _____

2.   Relationship Activities
(There can be overlap)

Hours

Talking with each other
about the relationship   _____

Service together   _____

Recreation shared together
(e.g., gardening, tennis)   _____

_____   _____

_____   _____

_____   _____

_____   _____

3. Increased Relationship Time

Activity   *Hours*

    Week 1: Talks

_____   _____

_____   _____

_____   _____

_____   _____

    Week 2: Talks

_____   _____

_____   _____

_____   _____

_____   _____

    Week 3: Talks

_____   _____

_____   _____

_____   _____

_____   _____

Project 10: In Service Together

The purpose in life, then, is not the gratifying of appetites nor of any selfish desires, but it is that the entity, the soul, may make the earth, where the entity finds its consciousness, a better place in which to live . . . So you'd better be up and doing, keeping self in accord with God's laws. (4047-2)

The fundamental purpose of life, according to the Edgar Cayce material, is not achieved by pursuing self-oriented goals; it is in the giving to others, in service, that we find the greatest fulfillment. For this reason, one of the most powerful measures two people can take to enhance the quality of their relationship is to make shared service a part of their lives together. Working alongside each other can increase their motivation to serve and their joy in serving. Sharing this joy and developing a sense of mutual reliance as they strive toward a common goal can add to the strength and depth of the relationship.

Exercise

Choose a project that you and your partner are both interested in and that you can work on actively together. The general thrust should be to make the world a better place. Your activity might very well be a tiny part of a much larger project involving many more people. Spend an hour a week together on this project for a month. Perhaps the short list below will suggest some possibilities you might want to consider.

Examples:
- Working in an animal shelter
- Working in a shelter for the homeless
- Planting flowers in the community
- Cleaning an area of the community

Project 11: Appreciate the Process

Put into practice day by day that [which] *is* known. Not some great deed or act, or speech, but line upon line, precept upon precept, here a little, there a little. (257-78)

A special benefit I've received in working on this book has been to experience again my wife's enthusiasm over the process of building a relationship. This project has reawakened us to the importance and the potential of loving this process and appreciating the stage our relationship is at today.

We are living in times in which there is much emphasis on the past and, even more strongly, on the future. Within a relationship we can easily find ourselves focused on memories of yesterday and plans for tomorrow. Many of us tend to lose sight of the ancient wisdom that directs our attention to the present. Yet, learning to value and enjoy a relationship for what it is today can be particularly fulfilling. The secret lies in our attitude toward time.

Many years ago, while I was in college and caught up in a social life of drinking, fraternities, and peer pressure that was making me increasingly uneasy, I drove to the farm where my mother had spent her childhood. There I talked with an elderly aunt who was still living at the farm and whom I admired. She spoke about time and how we spend so much energy developing ways to save it; and then we become frustrated over what to do with all our time and misuse it. My aunt felt that there was too strong a focus on the future and on trying to get "there." We needed to achieve more of a balance between setting ideals and goals and appreciating (and, I would suggest, even learning to love) the process of moving toward them.

The message we receive through much of our mass media today, particularly in advertising, suggests that relationships should be one long string of golden moments, with life just moving from one breathtaking event to the next. This can lead us to feel restless, guilty, worried, or just plain frustrated as we experience the process and do the every-day work required between these high points. We may begin to wonder why our relationship is not as continuously exhilarating as the ones we see on TV.

In my opinion, the key to resolving this question is as important as any principle in this book. It involves three basic steps:

First, we need to accept that there is a building process in any healthy relationship.

Second, we can learn to love the building process and the practice itself. This point is consistent with the Zen philosophy of finding happiness in the commonplace, the little things. We can come to enjoy placing the building blocks of a healthy relationship.

Third, from the viewpoint of—or tool from—the Cayce readings, placing these building blocks involves choosing to manifest the fruits of the spirit. We can find joy and fulfillment in focusing on the process of magnifying these qualities in our relationships:

> . . . if ye would have life, ye must give it. If ye would have love, ye must show thyself lovely. If ye would have friends, ye must show thyself friendly. If ye would have peace and harmony, forget self and make for harmony and peace in thy associations. (1650-1)

Exercise

The qualities listed on pages 206 and 207 are identified in the Cayce readings as fruits of the spirit. In the first listing, circle a number from 1 to 5 that indicates how good you yourself are at expressing each attribute. Use a 5 to show that there is a great deal of this characteristic in your behavior toward your loved one, and a 1 to show a minimal amount. In the second listing, indicate how well you feel your partner manifests each quality. There are also spaces for you to record personal examples of occasions on which each one was shown.

One purpose of this exercise is to encourage you to try to improve your ability to build those fruits of the spirit that you feel you are weakest at expressing. But an even more important goal is for you to focus on and come to appreciate and enjoy the process of building these qualities in your relationship.

Kindness   1 2 3 4 5   Kindness   1 2 3 4 5
Examples: _____   Examples: _____

_____   _____

_____   _____

Gentleness   1 2 3 4 5   Gentleness   1 2 3 4 5
Examples:_____   Examples: _____

_____   _____

_____   _____

Patience   1 2 3 4 5   Patience   1 2 3 4 5
Examples: _____   Examples: _____

_____   _____

_____   _____

Long-Suffering   1 2 3 4 5   Long-Suffering   1 2 3 4 5
Examples: _____   Examples: _____
_____   _____
_____   _____
_____   _____

Love   1 2 3 4 5   Love   1 2 3 4 5
Examples: _____   Examples: _____
_____   _____
_____   _____
_____   _____

Forgiveness   1 2 3 4 5   Forgiveness   1 2 3 4 5
Examples: _____   Examples: _____
_____   _____
_____   _____

Peacefulness   1 2 3 4 5   Peacefulness   1 2 3 4 5
Examples: _____   Examples: _____
_____   _____
_____   _____
_____   _____

Happiness   1 2 3 4 5   Happiness   1 2 3 4 5
Examples: _____   Examples: _____
_____   _____
_____   _____
_____   _____

Project 12: Using Pre-sleep Suggestions

The mental suggestions for the mental and physical and spiritual coordination would be by suggestions as the body loses itself in sleep . . . And as the body loses consciousness make those suggestions to the subconscious self that will take on, that will act . . . for a creative activity in the mental and spiritual forces of the body. (1188-1)

One of the fascinating recommendations in my grandfather's readings was given primarily for parents concerned about certain difficulties their children were having. In response to their questions, the readings described a process of pre-sleep suggestion that basically involved the parent talking with the child about the problem as he or she was going to sleep. The readings recommended this technique for a broad range of situations. These included fairly simple difficulties, such as straightforward learning frustrations and blocks in school; emotional/behavioral disorders like bed-wetting; and some problems that were much more complex. As a child psychologist, I have worked with hundreds of parents to help them use this process with their children, and I've found it to be a very helpful tool.

Pre-sleep suggestion has also proved quite valuable when used between adults in a relationship. It can help resolve a difficulty between the two of them, or it can enable either partner to work more successfully on a problem of his or her own.

For example, Leslie once used pre-sleep suggestion to help me through a particularly difficult time. My father had recently had a heart attack, and it had become necessary for me to take on a number of administrative responsibilities. This had created disturbances in my pattern of sleeping. I would wake up at night with my mind racing, thinking of all the problems that needed to be solved and the administrative decisions I had to make. I would become wide awake and find it difficult to get back to sleep.

The situation had worsened over a period of several months and I had tried various standard procedures to obtain help, but nothing worked. At this point Leslie proposed trying pre-sleep suggestion with me. We experimented with it for a few weeks, and the results were amazingly successful. I have talked with other adults who have used this technique with each other and who have met with similar success.

There are three basic parts to the pre-sleep suggestion process. In the first step, the person who will be giving the suggestions offers reassurances of love and support to the one who'll be receiving them.

In the second stage, the person giving the suggestions comments on the issue, being careful to phrase these remarks in the form of constructive alternatives to the problem. These alternatives might consist of possible attitude changes or changes in the way the listener responds to situations in which the difficulty arises.

The third aspect of the suggestion process involves further commentary on the situation. It is here that the suggestions are actually made. These should be given in a conversational tone, and rhetorical questions can be used. The point is not to issue commands to the listener or to make particularly forceful statements about how the problem must be met. The suggestions are to be given gently and positively. Some examples of how this can be done are included below in the description of the exercise.

Exercise

The first step of this exercise is for each person to describe on a separate sheet of paper an issue in the relationship that can be addressed using pre-sleep suggestion.

Next, the two people can work together to formulate an outline of a script (this can be very brief) to be used during the suggestion process. Each of the difficulties they've chosen to work on will require its own separate script. For each one, remember to follow the three-part format for the suggestions described above.

On alternate nights, each person gives the appropriate suggestions to the other. Delivering the suggestions in person is most effective; but, if this isn't possible, each partner can make a tape for the other about the issue he or she has decided to address. Here are six points to keep in mind as you give the suggestions to your partner:

1. Give the suggestions just as the other person is going to sleep. The important time seems to be the period that occurs between wakefulness and sleep, even though it may last just a few minutes. You will probably cover this critical interval if you give the suggestions over a fifteen-to-twenty-minute period beginning when the lights are out and your partner is relaxed and quiet, ready for sleep.

2. Give specific statements of reassurance, love, and support. I think sharing these feelings of connection actually forms a kind of energy bridge that allows for deeper, more effective communication between the two people. These statements of love and support might include brief descriptions of past experiences during which those feelings were mutually shared. Here is an example:

"Corinne, isn't it a great feeling when we are out in the yard doing chores together? I really enjoy your interest in nature and the way you care for the plants and animals. I hope you know how proud I am of you and how much I love you. You know I'm here to help you and to be a support. I especially appreciate how sensitive you are to other people. I feel that sensitivity toward me, too. I hope in our closeness you can feel my love and support. It sure seems to me that you are doing a great job of sorting out your interest in the different parts of your life. I know that sometimes it seems confusing, but I think you're doing a pretty good job."

3. Use the person's name in the suggestions, and if it's appropriate, touch the person while they are being given.

4. Phrase the specific suggestions so that the problem is mentioned, but a constructive alternative is given. For example:

"When you are not smoking, you feel better about yourself. You feel better about your body and more comfortable around other people when you are free from cigarettes. When you feel you need or want a cigarette, it sometimes helps to think about how good you feel about yourself when you choose to do something other than have a smoke. You have told me that when you are free from smoking, you feel you are more sensitive to other people and can think more clearly and creatively. The best thing is to take it one little step at a time, choosing to do something else when you feel you want a cigarette. I am really suggesting to you ideas that you have shared with me over and over—that you feel better and you know that you are healthier when you are free of cigarettes. It may be two steps forward and one step back sometimes, but you know that in the long run you are becoming free. From this time on, you are growing more and more determined in your attitude toward cigarettes. As this attitude gets stronger, it will be easier and easier for you to choose to be free of them." This kind of message can be repeated a number of times, with variations, over the fifteen-to-twenty-minute period. It is not necessary to use exactly the same words over and over. It does seem important for the person giving the suggestions to have discussed the situation ahead of time with the one receiving them and to include in the suggestions some of the receiver's own comments about wanting to change this part of his or her life.

5. Use positive statements. Do not use negative words such as *never, don't,* or *can't* in the suggestions.

6. Repeat the general suggestion at least five times, in order to allow your partner's subconscious to assimilate it.

Your Notes for Pre-sleep Suggestions

_____

_____

_____

_____

_____

_____

_____

Project 13: Being on the Same Wavelength

. . . are the thoughts, the activities, the desires, a complement one to another? . . . when these become as the mortise is to the tenon, as the copper is to the nickel . . . as the morning rays are to the dewdrop, *then* ye may know that such associations are chosen well. (440-20)

A number of the readings Edgar Cayce gave for couples stress the importance of each person being a complement to the other. If a relationship is to enable each partner to progress in the direction he or she wants to go, it is necessary that the paths of both have the same general heading. The association will be more fulfilling for each of them if they are able to work together toward goals that both consider worthwhile. For this to be possible, in at least some areas of their lives, the two people should be on the same wavelength with regard to what they want to accomplish in their relationship. This does not mean that they must have exactly the same priorities as each other. As the passage quoted above symbolically illustrates, it is not necessary for all the thoughts, activities, and desires of both partners to be identical; but there must be some points of contact, a compatibility of goals, if a man and a woman are to be able to combine their strengths and be effective helpmeets to one another:

The *law is, not* that ye may go one this way and the other that, and then your ideas and purposes be one; but where the treasure is, there may the heart be also, there may the activity be united. (263-18)

Exercise

The purpose of this exercise is to help you identify your own priorities in your relationship and reach a more complete understanding of your partner's. You'll be using a list of interests most typically involved in a relationship between husband and wife. The idea is to arrange the items in this list in their order of importance to you. In the blank to the left of each item, place the number from 1 to 12 that reflects the priority ranking you give that aspect of your relationship in comparison to the other eleven. Write the numbers from 1 to 12 in the blanks to the right as well, but in this column show what you expect of your partner. Don't try to guess how your partner will rank the items. Rather, use this as an opportunity to reflect your understanding of what his or her priorities actually are. Then, if possible, get your partner to complete the same two rankings of the items.

When you've both finished your lists, you'll find that they can furnish material for some very valuable discussion. Compare your rankings and talk them over with each other. Points you might want to discuss especially carefully include the differences in the priorities the two of you assigned the items, particularly the top five and the bottom five; your reasons for ranking the top five and the bottom

five as you did; and any sizable deviations between what
each of you expected from your partner and how the partner actually ranked the items.

Here is a list for you to use:

My Rank	Interests	My Partner's Rank
1. ___	To enjoy sex and be a satisfying sexual partner.	___
2. ___	To enjoy children and help in their care.	___
3. ___	To be a best friend.	___
4. ___	To organize and manage finances.	___
5. ___	To contribute in a significant way to community service projects.	___
6. ___	To be involved in community social activities.	___
7. ___	To nurture a small group of close, personal friendships.	___
8. ___	To contribute in a significant way to the family income.	___
9. ___	To have the primary responsibility for meals and housekeeping.	___
10. ___	To have close, good relationships with the in-laws.	___
11. ___	To have a significant ongoing connection with a church, temple, or other religious institution.	___
12. ___	To spend regular time and energy on spiritual disciplines.	___

Project 14: Being Whole with, Not Because of, a Relationship

The natural tendency of the entity . . . is to be the leader, the impelling influence. Do not let this, then, overshadow the abilities or the activities of the mate in *any* way or manner. This does not mean to become . . . subservient to his ideas; but let each give and take, knowing that this is to be a fifty-fifty proposition, with you each supplying that which is best within yourselves. (480-20)

A special type of balance is necessary in any healthy relationship. Both partners must be willing to merge with each other to a certain extent, to work together toward common goals; at the same time, each must maintain his or her own identity. In a sense, the inventory and comparison of priorities completed in the preceding exercise focused on the first part of this balance. In this project we'll be concentrating on the second element, the preservation of each person's individuality within a relationship. The willingness to give of oneself to one's partner, to forgo one's own desires if need be, is an important ingredient of a loving relationship. But this giving should not entail a sacrifice of either person's identity. On the contrary, for both partners to be able to contribute to their association, it's necessary that each have personal strengths to draw upon. Neither one can be completely dependent upon nor subservient to the other.

A certain amount of independence is needed, the ability to develop interests and associations outside the relationship that foster personal growth. Also necessary is the willingness to grant one's partner this same freedom to seek outside growth opportunities. When two people value their own and each other's individuality in this way, they are taking an important step in building a relationship that helps each of them in their efforts toward self-development.

Exercise

This exercise is designed to give you and your partner an opportunity to evaluate the extent to which your relationship contributes to your development as individuals.

Working separately, each of you should consider the following six questions about your relationship carefully. Take about an hour to arrive at your responses. Use a scale from 1 to 3 to indicate your answers: 1 would be used to show a no answer, 2 would correspond to sometimes or somewhat, and 3 would mean yes.

It can also be interesting to score the questions a second time, indicating how you think your partner will reply to them. When you have both finished answering the questions, spend an hour together discussing your responses.

1. Does each person have a secure belief in his or her own worth as a person?   1   2   3

2. Are both people improved by the relationship? Measured by some criterion from outside the relationship, are you better, stronger, more appealing, or more sensitive individuals?   1   2   3

3. Do you maintain serious interests outside the relationship, including meaningful personal associations with people other than your partner?   1   2   3

4. Is the relationship built into the other aspects of your life, rather than separate from them?   1   2   3

5. Are you jealous or uneasy about your partner's growth and expansion of interests?   1   2   3

6. Do you seek this person out for advice and sharing during difficult times?   1   2   3

Adapted from *Love and Addiction*, by Stanton Peele and Archie Brodsky, Taplinger Publishing Company, 1975.

A Concluding Note

In our Foreword to this work, we expressed the hope that this book would offer some helpful new insights toward making love relationships more personally gratifying and soul satisfying.

We hope that our shared experiences as a couple, as parents, and as active and participating students of the concepts in the Edgar Cayce readings have succeeded in transforming that hope into a reality for every reader.

"Love one another, but
make not a bond of love:
Let it rather be a moving sea
between the shores of your souls."

Bibliography

Cayce, Edgar, *The Edgar Cayce Library Series*, A.R.E. Press, Virginia Beach, Va., 24 volumes.

Cayce, Hugh Lynn, *Venture Inward*, Harper & Row, New York, N.Y., 1964.

Cerminara, Gina, *Many Mansions*, William Morrow & Company, New York, N.Y., 1950.

Colgrave, S., *The Spirit of the Valley: The Masculine and Feminine in Human Consciousness*, Tarcher, Los Angeles, Calif., 1979.

Fromm, E., *The Art of Loving*, Harper & Row, New York, N.Y., 1956.

George, Leonard, "The Case for Pleasure," *Esquire*, May 1989.

Gibran, Kahlil, *The Prophet*, Alfred A. Knopf, Inc., New York, N.Y., 1923.

Hall, Calvin, & Lindzey, G., *Theories of Personality*, John Wiley & Sons, Inc., New York, N.Y., 1970.

Jakoby, J., *The Psychology of C.G. Jung*, Yale University Press, New Haven, Conn., 1973.

Johnson, Robert A., *We: Understanding the Psychology of Romantic Love*, Harper & Row, New York, N.Y., 1983.

Jung, C. G., *Marriage as a Psychological Relationship in the Development of Personality*, Translated by R.F.C. Hull, Collected Works, Volume 17, Pantheon, New York, N.Y., 1954.

Keen, Sam, *The Passionate Life: Stages of Loving*, Harper & Row, San Francisco, Calif., 1983.

McGarey, William and Gladys, M.D.'s, *There Will Your Heart Be Also*, Warner Books, New York, N.Y., 1976.

Peck, M. Scott, *The Road Less Traveled*, Simon and Schuster, New York, N.Y., 1978.

Puryear, Herbert, *Sex and the Spiritual Path*, Bantam Books, New York, N.Y., 1986.

Rilke, R. M., *Letters to a Young Poet*, Translated by Steven Mitchell, Random House, New York, N.Y., 1984.

Sandford, John A., *The Invisible Partners*, Paulist Press, Mahwah, N.J., 1980.

Steiner, R., *The Gospel of St. John*, Anthroposophic Press, Hudson, N.Y., 1973.

Vissell, Barry and Joyce, *The Shared Heart*, Ramira Publishing, Aptos, Calif., 1984.

About the Authors

Charles Thomas Cayce, a child psychologist, graduated from Hampden-Sydney College, Hampden-Sydney, Virginia, in 1964 and received his doctorate from the University of Mississippi in 1968.

Since 1970 Dr. Cayce has lectured and taught throughout the United States and abroad on a variety of subjects that are addressed in the work of his late grandfather, the respected psychic Edgar Cayce. Dr. Cayce has authored numerous articles for journals and magazines and is the longtime president of the Association for Research and Enlightenment, Inc., and the Edgar Cayce Foundation, both nonprofit organizations headquartered in Virginia Beach, Virginia, and dedicated to researching and disseminating the Edgar Cayce work.

Leslie Goodman Cayce received her undergraduate degree from Antioch College in 1975 and her master's in social work in 1978 from Norfolk State College, in Norfolk, Virginia.

She is a clinical social worker at the Children's Hospital of the King's Daughters in Norfolk, Virginia.

Love Relationships: A Moving Sea is their first book.

What Is A.R.E.?

The Association for Research and Enlightenment, Inc. (A.R.E.®), is the international headquarters for the work of Edgar Cayce (1877-1945), who is considered the best-documented psychic of the twentieth century. Founded in 1931, the A.R.E. consists of a community of people from all walks of life and spiritual traditions, who have found meaningful and life-transformative insights from the readings of Edgar Cayce.

Although A.R.E. headquarters is located in Virginia Beach, Virginia— where visitors are always welcome—the A.R.E. community is a global network of individuals who offer conferences, educational activities, and fellowship around the world. People of every age are invited to participate in programs that focus on such topics as holistic health, dreams, reincarnation, ESP, the power of the mind, meditation, and personal spirituality.

In addition to study groups and various activities, the A.R.E. offers membership benefits and services, a bimonthly magazine, a newsletter, extracts from the Cayce readings, conferences, international tours, a massage school curriculum, an impressive volunteer network, a retreat-type camp for children and adults, and A.R.E. contacts around the world. A.R.E. also maintains an affiliation with Atlantic University, which offers a master's degree program in Transpersonal Studies.

For additional information about A.R.E. activities hosted near you, please contact:

A.R.E.
67th St. and Atlantic Ave.
P.O. Box 595
Virginia Beach, VA 23451-0595
(804) 428-3588

A.R.E. Press

A.R.E. Press is a publisher and distributor of books, audiotapes, and videos that offer guidance for a more fulfilling life. Our products are based on, or are compatible with, the concepts in the psychic readings of Edgar Cayce.

For a free catalog, please write to A.R.E. Press at the address below or call toll free 1-800-723-1112. For any other information, please call 804-428-3588.

A.R.E. Press
Sixty-Eighth & Atlantic Avenue
P.O. Box 656
Virginia Beach, VA 23451-0656